LIVING A
BIG WAR
IN A SMALL PLACE

LIVING A
BIG WAR
IN A SMALL PLACE

*Spartanburg, South Carolina,
during the Confederacy*

Philip N. Racine

The University of South Carolina Press

© 2013 University of South Carolina

Published by the University of South Carolina Press
Columbia, South Carolina 29208

www.sc.edu/uscpress

Manufactured in the United States of America

22 21 20 19 18 17 16 15 14 13   10 9 8 7 6 5 4 3 2 1

Library of Congress Cataloging-in-Publication Data

Racine, Philip N.
   Living a big war in a small place : Spartanburg, South Carolina, during
the Confederacy / Philip N. Racine.
     pages cm
   Includes bibliographical references and index.
   ISBN 978-1-61117-297-3 (pbk. : alk. paper) — ISBN 978-1-61117-298-0
(ebook) 1. Spartanburg County (S.C.)—History—19th century. 2. Spartanburg
County (S.C.)—Social conditions—19th century. 3. South Carolina—History—
Civil War, 1861–1865—History. I. Title.
   F277.S7R33 2013
   975.7'2903—dc23

                      2013013543

This book was printed on a recycled paper with 30 percent postconsumer waste content.

This book is for my students.

CONTENTS

ILLUSTRATIONS

ACKNOWLEDGMENTS

This small book is a distillation of material gathered over many years of studying and writing about the history of South Carolina and Spartanburg in particular. The contribution of the best of researchers, my wife Frances, to my last book, *Gentleman Merchants,* and this one is deep and invaluable. She found primary sources I surely would have missed. Since the material on which this book rests has been gathered over a forty year period, I owe many librarians and curators my deepest thanks. The debt goes far beyond that indicated in the endnotes and bibliography. Lastly, I thank my students for being so inquisitive about the story that is this book.

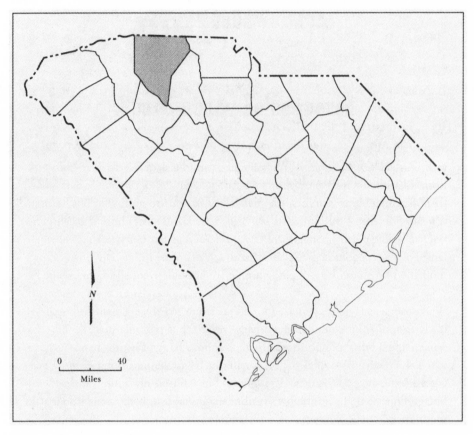

South Carolina. Map by Philip N. Racine, prepared by Spartan Photo Center.

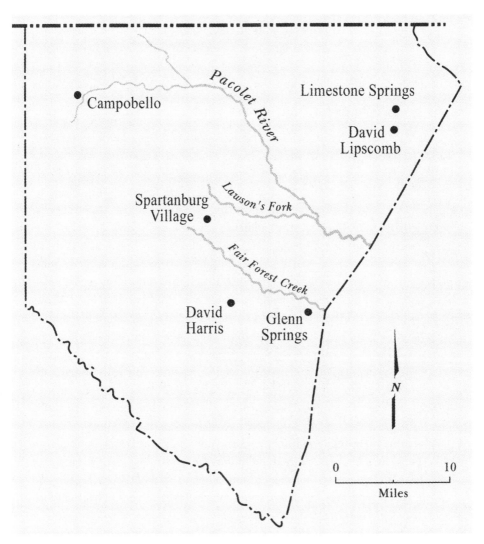

Campobello

Pacolet River

Limestone Springs

David
Lipscomb

Lawson's Fork

Spartanburg
Village

Fair Forest Creek

David
Harris

Glenn
Springs

N

0   10
Miles

Spartanburg District. Map by Philip N. Racine, prepared by Spartan Photo Center.

THE DISTRICT

PART ONE

People in Spartanburg District were in trouble. Life had become defined by scarcity, impossibly high prices, bad-tempered neighbors, and hard living. Many people were short on food. Salt, necessary to keep meat edible over time, was difficult to find and even then too expensive. Many lived in constant anxiety that a father or son off at war might be killed or wounded at any time. Often people blamed their troubles on their new government. Taxes were too high, everything cost too much and prices only seemed to get higher. What good news there was about the war seemed always to be followed by bad. The slave population was turning surly, and army deserters were threatening lawlessness—all creating fear. It seemed as if the new nation was on the brink of collapse, and leaders were asking for even more sacrifice, taxes, and fighting men, all resulting in more worry. How had such a good thing become so hard? How could their new nation, the Confederacy, and Spartanburg District survive? After starting off so well, so promising, so exciting, how had it all come to this?

1

The Setting

Located in the northwestern part of South Carolina among the foothills of the Appalachian Mountains, Spartanburg District is made up of rolling hills drained by three river systems: the Pacolet, the Tyger, and along its most northeastern border with York District, the Broad. In the antebellum period half of the adjoining county of present day Cherokee was part of Spartanburg District. Dotted by shoals and in the dry season, shallows, none of the rivers is navigable to the coast. Since the latter part of the eighteenth century the upstate had the majority of the state's white population and a minority of its black population. Some of South Carolina's lowcountry districts had populations that were 80 percent slaves while its upcountry districts had populations that were typically about 30 percent slaves. By 1860, the lowcountry was dominated by plantations. Coastal areas grew rice and cotton (on the sea islands and up to thirty miles inland planters grew the long fiber, silky, "sea island cotton" and the rest of the area grew inland, short staple cotton) while the upcountry districts grew corn, other grains, and the short fibered cotton. In Spartanburg District 56 percent of the heads of households owned their own land and 44 percent were tenants; overwhelmingly they grew grains, especially corn, and only a few bales of cotton. Only about 30 percent of the heads of households owned slaves, and almost all of those households grew cotton.

The center of the district was the city of Spartanburg. The city was more of a village. It had been laid out in 1787 on the Williamson plantation after its owner had sold the district a two-acre tract which contained a substantial spring.[1] The layout of the buildings was centered around a large rectangle of vacant land, which, in 1881, would become known as Morgan Square—named for the statue of Daniel Morgan erected to celebrate the one hundredth anniversary of his victory at the Battle of Cowpens.

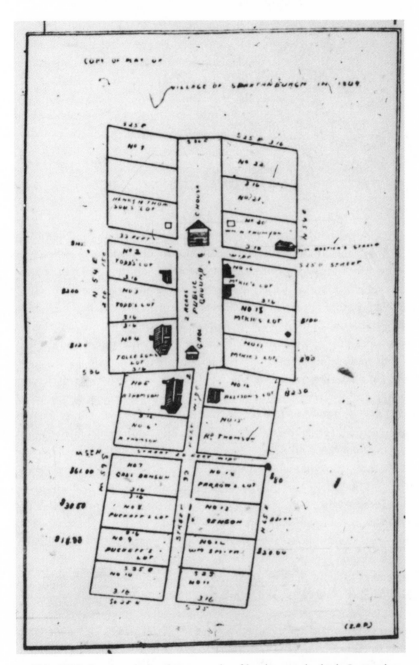

This 1809 drawing shows the rectangle of land around which Spartanburg village grew. Notice the jail on one end of the open space and the court house in the middle. Courtesy of Wofford College Library Archives.

At first the "square" was dominated by a jail on one end and a court house in the middle. By the 1860s, both had been removed; the court house (Spartanburg's third), was replaced in 1856 by an imposing structure with six two-story columns. Since 93 percent of the district's inhabitants were engaged in agriculture the village was small with one thousand to twelve hundred residents. In the mid 1850s, the *Carolina Spartan,* the village's newspaper, reported that the village consisted of "Thirteen dry-goods establishments; two saddler and harness establishments; two confectionary and druggist stores; one furniture room—any articles manufactured here; three carriage manufactories, five blacksmith shops; two shoe and boot making rooms; three tailoring establishments; three excellent hotels; three commodious churches, and another in progress of construction; two Academies, male and female; two day-schools for smaller pupils; lawyers and doctors a-plenty."[2]

By 1860 there were some changes: now there were nine lawyers, nine surgeons and dentists, fifteen more merchants, one watchmaker, one brick mason,

Built in 1850, the Palmetto House was one of three hotels in Spartanburg village during the Civil War. Photograph courtesy of the Herald-Journal Willis Collection, Spartanburg County Public Libraries.

several wealthy farmers and one college for males—Wofford College, established in 1854.[3] Spartanburg's business community grew little during the war. The Confederate government discouraged growing cotton, so agriculture stagnated. That same government bought up the production of the district's cotton mills, and other businesses had all they could handle supplying local demand. Many wealthy Confederates living elsewhere in the South late in the war nearly or actually bankrupted themselves by investing their fortunes in various Confederate bonds. It appears that the district's entrepreneurs did not as there was sufficient local capital after the war to promote and sustain a revived and expanded cotton mill building boom and a significant population increase in the city of Spartanburg.[4]

As to industry and manufacturing in the rest of the district, the 1860 Industrial and Manufacturing Census reported forty-six grist and saw mills employing fifty hands, six tanning establishments employing thirty-eight hands, six cotton mills employing sixty-two male hands and seventy-four female hands (continuing a tradition which dated back to the first of Spartanburg's mills which preferred female hands as mill owners considered them more careful with the thread, less likely to break it, and less likely to create labor troubles), one iron foundry, and four cotton gins. All these enterprises were small and supplied little more than the local market. Ultimately, trade outside of the district was in cotton grown by a few plantations and large farms—owners of small farms who were lucky enough to grow one or two bales sold them to their more substantial neighbors who blended them into their own larger crops.

The district also had seven male academies with 284 students and eight teachers, and two female academies with fifty eight students taught by two teachers. The census also listed forty-eight "primary schools," with a student population of 1,316 pupils taught by forty-eight teachers. The category "primary schools" probably included all the neighborhood, privately funded educational enterprises taught by tutors brought together by the individual efforts of farmers and businessmen. Year by year in their neighborhoods these people contracted with a teacher to instruct their children. David Harris, for instance, yearly tried to get up such a "school." He was not always successful, and some years his wife Emily would take on the extra burden of instructing their daughters and sons. Even these "home schooling" efforts may have been included in the category "primary schools."[5] Also listed were two "Male High Schools" with ninety pupils and four teachers, and two "Female High Schools" with 165 pupils and eighteen teachers. The relationship between these schools, if such existed, is somewhat unclear, but it is clear that they received little in public funding. Each of the academies and the primary schools received fifty dollars a year. Clearly these were privately funded schools.

The district also had a number of churches dominated by the dissenting denominations. The census listed thirty-four Baptist churches with 19,350 members, twenty Methodist churches with 6,987 members, two Presbyterian churches with 1,100 members, and two Episcopal churches with 850 members. The membership for the Baptist churches seems high (over two thirds of the entire population or more than the entire white population). Perhaps that membership included slaves. Many slave owners allowed and even preferred their slaves to attend church services, sometimes with, but most often separate from, the white members. Slaves often had their own preachers. These services with an all African-American congregation required the presence of a white person lest the preacher engage in unacceptable rhetoric. Slaves often preferred Baptist and Methodist services as they were more emotional than those of other denominations. Whether the African-American congregates were counted in the census totals for Baptist and Methodist churches is unknown. If they were it would help account for the exceptionally high number given as Baptist congregates.[6] In any case, the number was significantly exaggerated.

During the antebellum period, the politics of the district revolved around the Smith clan from the Southern part of the district. Its members were descendants of William Smith, who had served both as a United States Representative (1797–1799) and in the state senate (1801–1818). He had three sons, Isaac, John Winn who had his named changed to John Winsmith, and Elihu Penquite, all of whom served in the state house of representatives.[7] Dr. John Winsmith and his brother Elihu continued to buy land and slaves throughout the antebellum period until they became some of the wealthiest of Spartanburg's planters. John Winsmith and John Zimmerman, both of whom lived in the Glenn Springs area, owned the most slaves in the district—just over one hundred each. A significant challenge confronted the Smith clan's dominance in the district over the nullification issue in 1832. Most of the opposition to nullification came from the upstate districts, especially Pickens, Greenville, York, and Spartanburg. Among the leaders of the opposition to nullification in Spartanburg was James Edward Henry, who arrived in South Carolina in 1816 and went on to become one of Spartanburg village's leading lawyers and politicians. Indeed, Henry was usually on the opposite side of most political issues from the Smith clan. In the 1830s, the majority of the residents of Spartanburg opposed the Smiths and nullification. Over the years, however, the increased activity of Northern abolitionists and anti-slavery advocates drove the inhabitants of Spartanburg District—and even Henry—toward secession.

By the late 1840s as pressure for secession grew, especially in the deep South, all factions in the district were moving in a radical direction. This was illustrated by the appearance of both Dr. Winsmith and James Henry on the same platform at a public rally on March 6, 1849, where Winsmith, who chaired the meeting, told his audience: "the question is now urged as one of political power, by which it is intended to make every interest of the South—her labor, and all her industrial pursuits, entirely subservient to Northern supremacy. Under this aspect of the case, all will agree that it is high time, this agitating question was settled . . . it must be <u>met</u>, and met <u>now</u>."[8] Henry also spoke at this meeting, and his remarks were well received. Some days later, in a letter to a friend, he gave some indication as to why he had been so welcomed: "Will your state stand up to your resolves? If so we shall have a Southern Confederacy. <u>I have no doubt</u> I am willing to take my share of the <u>responsibility</u>. I hope my 'boys' in case of fighting will be ready to do their duty. . . . In fact I am not exactly certain but what a dissolution of the <u>Union</u> would be the best thing that could happen to us."[9] A compromise worked out by Henry Clay avoided South Carolina's secession in 1850, but the differences between the sections were too great, the anti-slavery forces too determined, the slavery system too uncompromising, and the moral issue of slavery too explosive for peace to last.

During the Civil War political alliances tended to form around personalities. The Whig party had disappeared, and the vast majority of citizens were Democrats, but party played almost no role in political affairs. Issues were either distinctly local or centered around support for or in opposition to the administration of Jefferson Davis. Figures who had become prominent in the politics of the district and whose influence would remain during the war were B. F. Kilgore and B. B. Foster among the farmers; Gabriel Cannon and Joseph Finger, who had industrial interests in the district; and H. H. Thomson, Hosea J. Dean, James Farrow, D. C. Judd, Joseph Foster, Simpson Bobo and O. E. Edwards among the village dwellers.[10] Residents of Spartanburg District elected the following delegates to the Secession Convention in December, 1860: John G. Landrum (Baptist minister), B. B. Foster (farmer), Benjamin F. Kilgore (physician-farmer), James H. Carlisle (professor of Mathematics at Wofford College), Simpson Bobo (lawyer) and William Curtis (Limestone Female High School president). Although a number of the district's inhabitants were unhappy with these proceedings, the overwhelming majority enthusiastically endorsed them.

Although the society of the district was generally egalitarian, there was no doubt that the wealthier farmers and townspeople were expected to lead, and so they did. Meta Grimball, an aristocratic refugee from the lowcountry, remarked on this seeming egalitarianism in the journal she kept during the Civil War.[11] Except in unusual circumstances such as secession, people left those interested in politics to engage in them at will. Farmers who owned middling land and few slaves often interacted with owners of thousands of acres and many slaves. David Harris, for instance, who owned ten slaves and four hundred acres, went hunting with Dr. John Winsmith who owned more than fifteen hundred acres and over one hundred slaves.[12] Most residents wished simply to be left alone and often showed remarkable apathy to the goings on in the district. Those persons, whether in the countryside or in the village, who seemed to have the most at stake when political decisions were made were happily obliged by the majority.

The entire state supported a slave economy. The lowcountry boasted its large plantations, with most having up to one hundred slaves, and many of the wealthy planters owned more than one plantation. The upcountry mainly consisted of small farms which typically had a smaller number of slaves (most often a slave family), and many farms with no slaves at all. Most upcountry people fervently supported slavery, for many upcountry, white, non-slave holders believed that the chief way to get ahead in the world was to acquire more land and obtain slaves. For many white people, the slave system was the bedrock of the greatest society the world had ever known, and many white people in South Carolina believed that any threat to the slave system was a threat to civilization itself.

Rural Spartanburg District was shattered by the Civil War. The relatively isolated area had a population of about twenty-eight thousand, about nine thousand of which were African Americans; Spartanburg village had about one thousand to twelve hundred inhabitants. The war years tested the mettle of these people, who were locked in a struggle that proved increasingly unpopular. After the Nullification controversy anti-slavery sympathies grew steadily in the rest of the nation (abolitionists were generally unpopular because of their insistence on the immediate eradication of slavery). After the nation acquired multiple territories in the West in the 1840s, Southern politicians became increasingly apprehensive over the issue of slavery's expansion into these newly acquired territories. This was a matter of principle more than reality, for few slave owners wished to move their slaves into what was then considered a desert. Southern politicians became exclusively defensive in their approach to national issues, and amidst this turmoil more residents of Spartanburg District mirrored their leaders and came to distrust the rest of the nation.

The major issue which overshadowed every other was slavery. From the 1830s on most of the white inhabitants of Spartanburg, both those who owned slaves and those who did not, grew increasingly defensive of their way of life. It appeared to them that the rest of the nation was determined to reduce the influence of their region and alter their institutions by ultimately abolishing slavery. This was ultimately symbolized in the second half of the 1850s by the rising strength of the Republican Party. In 1860, the election of a Republican president played a catalytic role in the secession of South Carolina from the Union. Defying the majority of their neighbors, some people in Spartanburg continued to reject secession as premature, unnecessary, and dangerous. Some Spartanburg residents were reluctant secessionists, primarily moved by public opinion. That reluctance would manifest itself in a myriad of ways during the coming war years. In the end, the war destroyed slavery, imperiled race control, and ultimately challenged the rural nature of life with an aggressive and voracious industrialism. The war profoundly shook the area's society. Spartanburg District was removed from the war's battles but not from its impact.

2

Spartanburg Wages War

S ecession from the Union meant the independence long sought after by many of the men and women of Spartanburg District. Others in the area were ambivalent about the Union for many years prior to the 1850s. Leaders of the pro-Union factions in South Carolina were for the most part upcountry people, but during the decade of the 1850s political events hardened the attitudes of the people of Spartanburg into a strong distrust of the northern and western parts of the nation. Secession, which almost everyone in Spartanburg District strongly supported, engendered a feeling of triumph and a certainty that they were right. David Harris, an owner of ten slaves and a four hundred acre farm, wrote in his daily journal: "The members of Congress (Some of them) says South Carolina shall be shipped back into the Union. As she has declared her independence, I had rather see her blotted out of existence than to apply for admittance in the union again. Let her stay out if she perishes for it. Let her die rather than so humble herself." Yet even before Fort Sumter made war certain, David had an uneasy feeling which lingered on behind his bravado: "As the certainty of war becomes more certain the fiery arder of the fighting men seems to cool off rapidly." For those whose love of the Union had remained steadfast this was a time for a brief last hurrah. For a few days a group of Union men from the Fair Forest Creek area just west of Glenn Springs formed a Union military company, but they soon disbanded in "fear [of] being hanged."[1]

Even though Spartanburg District supplied more troops to the war effort then its adjoining districts to the west (Greenville, Anderson, and Pickens), most of what followed affected all the districts. The leading proponent of Unionism in the upstate, Benjamin Perry, lived in Greenville, but even he gave in to public fervor and ultimately supported secession. These districts had problems with inhabitants that remained loyal to the Union, as well as deserters.[2] Those same upstate districts—including York, which had the highest number of military deaths per one thousand enrolled in the state—had similar characteristics and issues with the legislature, the army, and the lowcountry. The wartime story of these districts was much like Spartanburg's.[3]

"Rub up your Rifle the War has begun" William Camp wrote David Harris, his brother-in-law, in a note he left on Harris's kitchen table. "The fight Began yesterday Evening[,] a little before Night thar was 9 War Steamers hove in sight & they [the Union navy] Started one in to fort Sumter but it did not get there. Our batterys opened upon it & then Sumter opened on our batteries. The vessel turned back to Sea and then our Guns were turned on Sumter . . . . The highest state of Excitement prevails in Spartanburgh Just Now and thare is considerable Slinging of Snott."[4] Camp's vulgar phrase was a nineteenth century description of blowing the nose with the fingers, a gesture which showed utter disdain when aimed at anyone or anything—in this case, Yankees. Camp reflected his contempt for the North and typified the attitude of many Southerners toward their enemy. After Sumter, April 1861, it was war. As the last states joined the Confederacy cannons boomed in Spartanburg, as they did throughout the South, to tell the people.

In the few months after Sumter, but before the fighting commenced, most people were euphoric and somewhat apprehensive. Many had not expected the Northern states to go to war over slavery and secession and therefore were surprised when President Lincoln called out seventy-five thousand volunteers to defend the Union. With the news of the first battle a strange mixture of emotions—joy and grief, bluster and fear, elation at one moment and despair at the next—began to settle in on the people. At times, fear and a premonition of possible disaster intruded on people's general optimism, and they began "to feel that it is a dreadful reality, that we are in the midst of a desperate war, and no one can tell when it will end. It is bad, very bad." But in the next instant the pride and bravado took over: "Let us fight on to the last man."[5] The first military engagements were glorious victories enhanced by the stirring firsthand accounts delivered by "veterans" on the public square. These appearances by Spartanburg's finest flower of manhood heightened spirits and turned out many to volunteer. As is true of most wars, people in the district thought the conflict, though fraught with danger, would be a short and brave adventure.[6]

The village of Spartanburg was the political and financial center of the district, and so it became the focus of war activity. During the tense months preceding the bombardment of Fort Sumter villagers worried about possible fifth column movements. They kept a keen eye open for Union sympathizers, abolitionists, and strangers. The city council increased the night watch to keep the peace, guard against those who might wish to set fires and otherwise do damage, and mounted extra patrols to ride the district roads and check on people who were out late at night. An uneasiness seemed to permeate the atmosphere, a feeling which remained well after events at Fort Sumter. Once war was certain, the district became a flurry of activity. The state ordered all of its arms, loaned to or otherwise, in the possession of local militia to be collected and accounted for. It also took over the iron works in York and Spartanburg Districts and set them to casting cannon.[7] The Confederate government enlisted into its services other industries in the area which had value to the war effort. Dexter Converse, who had come to Spartanburg from the North in the 1850s and volunteered for Confederate army service, was instructed to continue running his Bivingsville Cotton Mill on the Pacolet river. The mill would supply the Confederate army with cloth for uniforms. Although people took notice of all of this activity, it did not mask the apprehension they felt about the traitors and agitators they imagined in their midst.

Of all the causes for concern voiced by people in the district, there was one fear which dominated all of the rest. The district's weekly newspaper, the *Carolina Spartan,* wrote of what was really bothering the people in Spartanburg when it warned that if normal war measures did not suffice to bring the North victory, then "insidious influences, through spies and disloyal citizens, are to be exerted [by the Union] upon our colored population. . . . Flames, swords, poisons by their own hands, or through your contented domestics, will all be used." There it was: a real danger lay in the possibility of slave rebellion, either by stealth or in open revolution. The paper wrote that the people of Spartanburg should:

> flatter not ourselves that there is no danger. We know not who are in our midst, that may enter into the heart of our Blackamoors, and there drop a motive that shall fester late deeds of violence. We know not what a tide of influences may pour in from disaffected sections in adjoining states, or through persons who wear the badge of loyalty, but, in the heart, lodge secret motives of enmity, ready at any time to burst forth in a broad and extended devastation. So far as we are able to decide just now, the prospect of internal dangers does not seem to be imminent. While the surface looks calm, we know not what under currents may flow, which, by their gathering heat and intensity, will agitate society from its base to its cap stone. Is it not our duty then, to anticipate danger and guard against it?

The paper hysterically drew pictures of what might happen, calculated to frighten the most sanguine of people and even went on to call for vigilante action: "Let no suspicious person pass without a rigid examination, let no utterance of doubtful loyalty go unexamined—let no trades men or salesmen . . . hailing from any disaffected section of the country . . . pass without requiring the fullest evidences that [they are] . . . genuine. To do this, let committees be formed voluntarily, if not by authority, whose duty it shall be to . . . report to our local State Authorities. . . all persons, whether transient or local, who, by act or speech, render themselves obnoxious to the charge of disloyalty."[8] It is true that the possibility of a slave insurrection crossed almost everyone's mind early in the war, but there was no evidence to support the suspicion. The slaves were, on the whole, quiet. They did not have much choice, for they were under as complete control as ever. Patrols were suspicious of travelers in Spartanburg and often stopped and questioned them, but there were no cases of anyone being found disloyal. The fact was that Spartanburg was too small and isolated to attract Union spies.[9] The newspaper was giving voice to the hysteria of people who found themselves in new and frightening circumstances.

The village did mount a local militia group, and it did have at least one "call to arms." William Kennedy Blake, the principal of the Spartanburg Female College, described the event in his recollections:

In the early part of the war, a company for home defence was organized in the town. Prof. DuPre [who taught at the recently founded Wofford College] was the captain and among the members were Dr. Shipp [also from the Wofford faculty], Dr. Boyd, J. W. Vandiver and other dignified seniors. For awhile the company drilled in the courthouse, but soon they went through their evolutions on the street, where some rich things occurred to the amusement of the lookers on. Dr. Vandiver was the source of a great deal of fun. Those who knew him will recall his long stride which he never varied and which defied all measure of time. On one occasion while marching single file, the officer in passing Dr. V. observed that he was out of step and remarked "Dr., you are not in step with your file leader," Dr. V. very drily replied "Hardly ever am." And added, "If it hurts your feelings you had better get the other fellers to keep step with me!" A few weeks later news was brought to Spartanburg that the raiders who had been committing serious depradations in Polk County N. C. and in the Jackson Neighborhood in Spartanburg county, were expected to make an attack on Fingerville, a village just beyond New Prospect. It was decided that the Home Guards should go to the rescue of the people in that neighborhood: Orders were issued and by noon some forty men were in the saddle, armed and equipped for the march. We reached Fingerville about dusk: here the force was divided: some twenty men remaining for the defence of Fingerville while the remainder undertook a scouting expedition in search of the raiders. I was in command of the latter party, and with Henry Alley and one of the Jacksons as pilots, we began the tramp. After a long and diligent search through the mountains and valleys of Polk county, we arrived at the house of a widow Jackson about daylight: There we stopped and rested and had served us an excellent and most acceptable breakfast: The raiders had evidently got word of our movements and had retired to their hiding place in the mountains. After breakfast we resumed our saddles and making a wide tour came into the Howard Gap road not far from where Landrum station is located. Finding no trace of the raiders, we concluded to return to Spartanburg. While riding leisurely down the Howard Gap road, Dr. Shipp, Dr. Boyd and myself being in advance of our party,—we saw a man on foot with a gun on his shoulder approach us. When several hundred yards distant he stopped, and after a short pause, took to the woods. Dr. Shipp exclaimed "A Raider!" and spurring his horse, dashed through the woods to head him, calling to him to halt. But he did not halt worth a cent, and Dr. S-, seeing that he was about to make good his escape, discharged both barrels of his shot gun as a reminder to the poor fellow that he was badly wanted. He was doubtless some deserter, who, being on foot, had the decided advantage of those who pursued him, the thick undergrowth retarding the advance of the horses and enabling him to get away without difficulty. When we reached Spartanburg we found that the other detachment of our company had already arrived, and upon the roll being called it was found that whatever else the expedition had cost, there was not a man either killed, wounded or missing.[10]

There were several places in the district where the inhabitants formed home guards. On the main stage line between Spartanburg and Greenville, two successful schools, one for male students and one for female students, were founded by the Rev. R. H. Reid. The two schools were part of the district's only "planned community" which was called Reidville. Citizens of Reidville petitioned the governor: "students of the Male School are under Military discipline, having daily drills, under the supervision of the Principal Mr Capers. . . . The Citizens have organized a Home Guard, which meets and drills every two weeks. . . . In order that we may be enabled to afford protection to the property and lives of the citizens, we respectfully petition your Excellency for the use of State arms, i.e. Fifty Muskets and accoutrements." The petition was accompanied by an endorsement from Representative James Farrow in which he stated: "The Community of Reidville is one in which should we have domestic troubles at all they would be as likely to arise trouble there as anywhere also in our District there being in that community a large proportion of slaves with comparatively a small number of adult males— many soldiers from that region having gone into the Confed. Service."[11]

All these efforts were in vain. For the people of Spartanburg District there would be no combat; their fields would not be turned into battlegrounds. The battles would be something going on somewhere else; not that there were not great sacrifices demanded of the people, nor that they would not appreciate what war meant—there would be too many local men dead and maimed for that. What drama and heroism marked the experience of the Civil War in Spartanburg District was not that of the battlefield, but was evident in the lives of village and farm people desperately and quietly trying to deal with changes that threatened to overwhelm them. Some people managed and some failed in isolation, while others sought some measure of control over their changing lives, fruitless though that effort came to seem, in the comfort of groups.

The district experienced combat vicariously through the lives of its soldiers. Many soldiers, leaving farm, factory, and school, moved quickly to volunteer. As the war dragged on there would be two regiments which had five companies of Spartanburg men (regiments normally were made up of ten companies). One company called the Spartanburg Rangers was made up of seventeen-year-old re-cruits from the district. In all, Spartanburg District supplied thirty-three compa-nies. In addition, men from the district were scattered in various companies from all over the state. Three to four thousand district men served in military units, including the state militia. In the end Spartanburg District suffered the fourth highest casualty rate per one thousand men of all the districts in the state. The two regiments formed in the district were the thirteenth regiment, South Carolina Volunteers under the command of Oliver E. Edwards, the law partner of Simpson Bobo. Edwards was later killed at the battle of Chancellorsville, and replaced by colonel Benjamin Brockman. The second regiment was called the Holcombe Le-gion which was commanded by colonel P. F. Stephens. These two regiments and most of the companies from Spartanburg served in Virginia under Robert E. Lee, although a few companies served in the western part of the Confederacy.[12]

Although the district was not located near any battles or even major move-ments of troops, the residents of the area learned of military matters from the telegraph, the railroad, and especially from the *Carolina Spartan*. The *Spartan* was a weekly newspaper which published stories taken from national newspa-pers, other South Carolina newspapers, and from a few of its own imbedded correspondents as well as correspondence it received directly from Spartanburg soldiers and their families. During 1861, the *Spartan* took obvious pride in the number of the district's residents who had enrolled, providing the following in its October 10th issue:

> List of Companies from Spartanburg District, So. Ca.
> now in the service of the Confederate States:
>   5th Regiment, Col. Jeffries
>   The Spartan Rifles, Capt. Jos. Walker

The Morgan Infantry, Capt. A. H. Walker
Lawson's Fork Guard, Capt. B. B. Seay
Company O, Capt. J. Q. Carpenter
13th Regiment, Col. O. E. Edwards
The Forrest Guard, Capt. D. R. Duncan
The Pacolette Guard, Capt. W. P. Compton
The Cherokee Guard, Capt. W. B. Wofford
The Brockman Guard, Capt. Brockman
The Iron District Volunteers, Capt. A. K. Smith

In 1861 the paper regularly published lists of soldiers from the district who had been killed. As the war ground on it did so less frequently until 1864, when it once again began to publish the long lists of those killed.[13] The paper also increased its war news during 1864. The newspaper reflected the growing concern about the course of the war when it reported on July 28, 1864:

> At this meeting, it was resolved that citizens of this district immediately organize a regiment to be held in readiness, should any emergency arise, to welcome our ruthless invaders "with bloody hands to hospitable graves." . . . We should not fold our arms in fancied security. . . . That there may be no misapprehension as to the object of the organization, we will state that the Regiment is independent of and distinct from any Confederate or State forces, and has no connection with the Militia or Conscript forces, but simply intended as an organization around which every man in the District, (old and young) able to shoulder a gun may rally should occasion require it, to repel the invasion of our homes.[14]

The regiment was to be named "The Lawson's Fork Home Guards."

So unprepared for war was the state that the first regiments formed were without side arms, such as the thirteenth South Carolina Regiment, which elected O. E. Edwards its colonel.[15] The men who made up these regiments were not soldiers and knew nothing of military discipline, and enthusiasm could not always make up for a lack of training. What little preparation local recruits received in Spartanburg provided some amusement to the more skeptical lookers on: "It was amusing to see the action of the soldiers. They leaped up, leaped backwards, sideways, turned one way then the other, squatted, stopped, jumped, snorted, spit shut their eyes, bowed and scraped, and looked very monkeyish." Though amateurs, the men were excited and eager to get into battle and displayed great zeal when told they would be going to Charleston. One onlooker captured the somewhat comic atmosphere in a comment he made when he saw "more soldiers on their way to Charleston (several thousand to take on sixty). They will charge down to Charleston then charge back again."[16]

After Sumter, the soldiers knew it would be real war. Along with three of his brothers, Eliphas Smith, son of Elihu P. Smith of Glenn Springs, a prominent planter and slave trader, volunteered early for the conflict. He was a faithful correspondent who wrote his mother often, sometimes taxing her by demanding frequent letters in return. He seemed to forget she had three other sons in the army to write to. Eliphas was caught up in the splendor, excitement, and romance of the first few months of war. On his way to Virginia with his regiment he described and exulted in the greetings they received: "At Charlotte our reception was beyond any things you can imagine when the whole concourse of ladies and gentlemen turned out and showered flowers upon us bidding us welcome to their state. The most splendid dinner was served to us I ever have enjoyed. The young ladies waited upon us."[17] The euphoria evident here was typical of the first months of the war. The celebrations and excitement would eventually be blasted by the realities of camp life and combat.

After the first battle at Manassas in July of 1861, Eliphas had a different view of the war. In August he wrote one of his sisters: "I have made up my mind to bravely face every danger for my country's sake, & If I fall in the conflict I cannot die in a better cause. Four of your brothers are now in [the] field[;] all can't survive the conflict. Some of us will either get wounded or killed, no doubt you may as

Captured Confederate winter encampment. Courtesy of the Library of Congress, Prints and Photographs Division.

well make up your minds for such an occurrence; & never will you hear anything derogatory to any of their characters." Eliphus was deeply affected by his battle-field experience, and although his letter was typical in its reference to upholding the honor of his family, it was not typical in another more sinister aspect.

Writing so early in the war and after only one battle Eliphas showed a mature and keen understanding of what war could mean when he wrote that in the army "a man loses all the feeling for fellow men. I have seen men die in the most excru-ciating manner [and] never even so much as ask who he is. I have become callous as to death, all men will become so, even brothers are indifferent to one another's death."[18] Though perhaps somewhat overstated in the wake of his first battle, Eliphus had seen a profound truth. Yet such a letter was not calculated to soothe and quiet the apprehensive fears of his two teenage sisters in Glenn Springs. They must have shivered when they read it.

Service in the army was unpleasant for everyone, but for some it was more bearable than for others. A few Spartanburg officers took servants with them, and at times the slaves made contracts among themselves to divide the time they would spend in service to their masters in the ranks. A slave serving on James Island near Charleston wrote to his wife: "Tell Elihu [another slave] it was his request that we should divide our time in the War. He must write before I come home if he is still of the notion. If he is we will divide the time, not that I am tired of the war but it was the contract."[19] The common soldier, however, had to fend for himself. Letters home told of long lonely hours on picket duty, standing in the cold and the wet, and sleeping on the ground without any cover. These letters also warned friends to beware enlistment for "the man who volunteers thinking it a frolick will find fun different to his expectations."[20] Soldiers, searching for ways to ease the boredom of camp life, often took to drinking liquor. Many young men, unaccustomed to hard drink, developed a taste for it in the army. Demand drove up the price and soldiers sought a supply from home. For some, the antipathy to strong drink among relatives created problems. Eliphas Smith wrote his mother: "I wrote for a little Jug of Spirits to be sent & as you seem to be fearful of the con-sequence of intoxicating drinks, perhaps you had better not send it. I assure you we never drink." If "we" was meant to imply the whole regiment, it was a strange regiment indeed. At times, necessity and the needs of health came to the rescue of a boy's reputation at home: "Our mess has got quinine to take for the preven-tion of fever. The Surgeon recommends that it be taken in brandy or whiskey. I want you by all means to send some of this brandy if you have it. Two or three gallons would not be too much. . . . Be sure and not forget this as we cannot take our quinine until we get the brandy. You need not let anybody know this for they will say that we have turned out to drinking. The best way to send it would be to put it in the box of provisions."[21] For whatever purpose, medicinal or otherwise, spirits were always welcome.

For those men who did not volunteer for Confederate service during the first year of the war, the pressure to do so soon mounted. Men who had volunteered early for six months' service became disillusioned with the war. The reality of death, the mean, dirty existence of camp life, and the loneliness and boredom of long periods of inactivity discouraged others from volunteering, and the ranks became dangerously thin. In April 1862 the Confederate Congress passed the first conscription law in American history, making men between the ages of eighteen and thirty-five eligible for the draft.[22] Many people were caught unawares, for the draft had been considered unthinkable some months before. Many Southerners had believed that patriotism alone would keep the ranks filled. Now faced with the draft, young men were likely to volunteer since that allowed them to choose service with either the artillery, cavalry (if they could provide their own horses), or infantry. A conscript or draftee got no such privilege. Another option was to volunteer for service in the state militia which states jealously protected for home defense. Yet the new laws did not ensnare everyone, for both the conscription laws of South Carolina and the Confederacy provided for exemptions. These applied to men who owned twenty or more slaves, and were galling to those in Spartanburg District who owned small numbers of slaves, or none at all. South Carolina law exempted any white resident who oversaw any group of slaves larger than nineteen, whether overseer or owner. Everyone else had to register for the draft by signing the conscription roles.

Although service in the military now seemed inevitable for most young men in Spartanburg, many did not exercise the option to volunteer, preferring instead to gamble on the off chance that they might not be called up. If they lost and were drafted they had to bear the derision of their neighbors, for many people in the district considered conscripts the "crew that does not want to fight for their country." Draftees left the village by train "with as good grace as possibl." By July 1862, the need for manpower had become critical, and the Confederacy required men thirty-five to forty-five years old to enroll in a state unit, organize themselves, and go into camp for military training. The results were not pleasing to either the men in the camp or to the instructors.[23]

David Golightly Harris, age forty-one, was among those who volunteered for six months' service in a state militia unit in 1862. Although he professed what verged on contempt for conscripts, his was a position not too far removed from theirs. He did not enroll until there was no choice left. When, in December 1861, the legislature made all males sixteen to forty-five years old eligible for the draft into the South Carolina militia for six months' service, it also provided that

David G. Harris. Courtesy of Wofford College Library Archives.

a man could volunteer when his name came up for conscription.[24] When David's name was drawn he wrote, somewhat lamely: "the time has come for all such as me to go to the field & do our part for the defence of our Country. It will be a bitter [pill] for me to take. But it had as well be me as any one. Every-one should do his part[;] there is need for *all* that *all* can do. I thought that those that was willing to fight for money, and those who went from ambishous motives, should go first."[25] At least Harris went when asked. Many men in the district who were drafted into Confederate service or enrolled into state service did not leave when they were supposed to but straggled behind. Harris's commander sent him back to Spartanburg to round them up. Harris served his six months and returned to his farm. In July of 1863, he was made eligible for conscription into Confederate service and given two weeks to volunteer before being conscripted. He served about two months and then hired a substitute.

Hiring substitutes was a less than popular but not quite dishonorable practice. For money or land a young man otherwise exempted from service could be hired to replace a conscripted soldier. In some cases the substitute served only a part of a man's time, and in others he served the full term. There were many reasons for hiring substitutes. In Harris's case, he felt that he could not be spared from his farm for those three months. Other men just wanted out from the filth and horror of war and camp life. One Spartanburg officer complained:

I can hardly write the gnats are so bad. Sandflies are also very bad. I want to get to a place where such things are unknown. I had hoped before this to have got a letter from you saying that you had procured me a substitute. What is the matter? Have you tried or are none to be had. I have just learned today of a man who is anxious to substitute. His name is Billy Edwards. He [lives] near Buck Bennets. I want you to go and see him immediately for if I get one the sooner the better and if I keep waiting long enough the war will be ended. Maybe I do not offer money enough. In price you may go as high as 2500. dollars. Perhaps you may strike a trade with Edwards. Some men will come for the money or land or whatnot you promise to give. Perhaps you can get him for a good deal less. I want you to go see [him] the first day you get this letter and write me so I may know what to expect. Make everything look as favorable as possible. Tell him that our brigade will be apt to stay in S. C. til the war ends. . . . I could not endure these biting insects for a thousand dollars or so.[26]

By 1863, substitutes were not only hard to get, but expensive as well. In general, whether men were substitutes, conscripts, or volunteers they fought, if not willingly, at least well. The legend of the Confederate soldier is well entrenched and need not be reviewed here. It might be well to remember, however, that he came from places like Spartanburg District, brought up on its farms and nurtured on its past.

From the early months of the war many people in the district sought ways in which they could contribute to the war effort. Having soldiers from Spartanburg in the field meant that the community could help provide them with clothing and other material support, it could comfort and support the families of the wounded and dead, and it could help families cope with the absence of the one man on whom their livelihood depended. The need for homemade goods to help support the army was acute because the South was sorely lacking in manufacturing. What manufacturers had existed prior to the outbreak of the war were on the whole small, and most had supplied only local markets. Among the efforts in Spartanburg to augment the output of these industries was the formation of the Methodist Relief Society in July, 1861, "having for its object the relief of the sick and wounded soldiers of our army."[27] The society met weekly and assigned various types of garments to be made by the membership. By December of 1861, the members had made eighty-eight shirts, fifty-two socks, twenty-nine pairs of drawers, thirty-five sheets and many other assorted items. The society sold fancy items, such as lace handkerchiefs, and used the money they raised to buy material with which to make clothing for the soldiers. The society sent boxes of stores to

Spartanburg men in Virginia and medical supplies to Columbia, South Carolina. The delicacy of certain ladies was offended when they were asked to send partly worn men's undergarments, but the local newspaper, the *Carolina Spartan,* contended that "there is no room for such scruples." The newspaper quoted from a soldier's letter in which he wrote of boxes "from home, containing amongst other articles, partly worn, under garments, and they were greatly needed. Nothing seems to do a poor sick soldier as much good, as a *suit of clean under* clothes. Many a lip murmured 'God bless the ladies of Spartanburg.'"[28]

The "ladies of Spartanburg" became discontented, however, when they learned that their supplies were not being reserved for soldiers of South Carolina. The society wrote Governor Andrew Pickens that they wished the goods they had made to be used only by the troops of their state. In this instance, they were reflecting one of the greatest problems faced by the Confederacy. Southerners identified more with their states than with their new national government, the Confederate States of America. The petty jealousies inherent in that situation sorely taxed the patience and diplomacy of nationally-minded Confederates. In a letter to Whiteford Smith, the secretary of the Methodist Relief Society, the Secretary of the Treasury of the Confederacy, C. G. Memminger of South Carolina, apologized with a touch of sarcasm: "The Quartermaster General deeply regrets the impression made upon the minds of the patriotic ladies of Spartanburg as to the disposition made of their supplies. In several instances packages have been forwarded . . . without the proper information, as to who the contributors were, and the direction desired to be taken by the articles contributed. In such instances the packages have been placed among the general stores of the Department, and issued to the soldiers most in need."[29] Secretary Memminger may have been irked that even among the vaunted zeal of the "ladies of Spartanburg" patriotism had its limits. Such groups of local people formed all over the district. The *Spartan* reported their formation almost weekly for months. And most did not share the peculiar scruples of the Methodist Relief Society. The *Spartan* reported that the boxes of another relief society, formed on August 29, 1861, would be sent to Richmond, and its representative there said that "He will fill requisitions not only for the use of South Carolinians, but for all Confederate soldiers, as far as in his power."[30]

There is no doubt that the supplies donated by local relief groups were important to the war effort. With the federal blockade of the Southern coast, supplies became increasingly critical, and the efforts made by those at home to supply those in the field were heroic. The *Carolina Spartan* published stories of hardship at the military camps and reported on the progress of local relief groups as an indication of how united the population was in its support of the war. Pointing out that it was customary for representatives of relief organizations in Spartanburg to meet troop trains arriving in the village to inquire as to their needs, the *Spartan* related one incident which showed not only the patriotism of the white ladies but also attempted to demonstrate the support for the war among slaves. It seems that troops on one train needed blankets and "a servant, named Louise, belonging to Mrs. Jesse Cleveland, brought to one of the ladies of the family a fine, large white blanket, and asked her if she thought it would be accepted. When asked if that was not the fine blanket her master gave her before his death (more than ten years) she replied that it was, and she thought so much of it she had *never used* it; but if a soldier, who was going to fight for us, would accept it, she wanted him to have it. It was accordingly sent and accepted."

The *Spartan* also delighted in reporting any incident of loyalty or service by slaves who were body servants to their masters on battle fields. The *Spartan* added the following to its reporting on the incident with the blanket: "A body servant followed his master into a fight and was told to hide behind a large tree for fear of his being easily killed to which he answered: 'No Sir, I can't stay here. I came with Mass Eddie, and I *am going to stay right beside him as long as I live, and he lives.*' He kept his word. Through the whole of this fearful day, he never faltered, in his devotion to the youth, whose cradle he had rocked, and his conduct is the adoration of the whole Regiment." The newspaper took special delight in commenting: "New York Herald, Times, Tribune, please copy and make a note of this in getting up plans for insurrections."[31] Although probably written in an offhand manner, the comment about insurrections reflects a subliminal if not overtly conscious anxiety about the possibility of a slave revolt instigated by Yankee infiltrators.

Being able to supply clothing and blankets was rewarding, but it did not fulfill the desire to aid with the ultimate disasters of war—the wounding and killing of men. Although Spartanburg was not located near any battlefield, the citizens wanted to tend to the sick and wounded. One way of doing so was to raise much needed money for medical supplies. The most pleasant method was to put on amateur theatricals and concerts which provided much needed entertainment and diversion from the privations everyone felt. One such gala affair boasted twenty-one different presentations of singing and instrumental music with quartets, piano solos, trios, and choruses.[32] The funds raised in this fashion also helped to support William Walker, a local man serving as a nurse in Virginia (nursing had not as yet become a "woman's" profession), and the author of *Southern Harmony,* a widely used book of hymns.

Walker's letters to the Methodist Relief Association gave its members a feeling of being a part of the nursing of their soldiers, and it in turn made South Carolina boys, and those from Spartanburg in particular, feel as if they had direct support from home. Walker was a dedicated man who made a particular effort to send back news of every wounded Spartanburg soldier he came across in his travels from hospital to hospital. He found conditions hard—"a great increase of sickness mostly Typhoid Fever and diareah which are the scurge of our Armies"—and bandages and lint in short supply. He reported that the soldiers had been especially pleased with a recent package from Spartanburg: "the port wine and whiskey have been of great service but nothing more needed than blackberry wine which is hard to get from the great scarcity of sugar." Walker was widely known in the ranks and among the officers for careful and conscientious work: Spartanburg was well represented in him. He could just as well have been speaking of himself when he wrote: "Ladies, I feel glad to be able to inform you that your labor is highly appreciated not only by our soldiers [but] by the public generally, and by the Authorities I am known as the Spartan Ladies Agent (the only one here) and hence I receive favors and am admitted as a nurse to privileges . . . others are not allowed."[33]

The wounded eventually returned to Spartanburg. The relief societies in the village met the trains each day and provided the soldiers with meals and makeshift hospital facilities in large rooms rented in town. Teams of two women took turns working in these hospitals, caring for the wounded for one week at a time. There were other citizens of the village who provided spare rooms or who fed several soldiers in addition to their own families. They gave rest, care, and shelter to many who were too weak after a long train ride to journey home immediately. What little money or possessions people had they were willing to share, and all were amply rewarded by the soldiers who "when bidding us goodbye, showed, by the grasp of the hand, and often times by tears, how gratefully they appreciated an act of kindness to a stranger." In these selfless ways many who had to remain behind in the village did something direct and useful for the war effort.[34] As the years passed, doing anything at all for the wounded, even something trivial, took on added significance for villagers as they realized how helpless everyone was in the face of the mounting death toll. As late as 1864 there was a communication to the *Spartan* on the good being done by the ladies of Spartanburg who hoped to establish "A Soldier's Wayside House." The newspaper stated that "there is no place surely in the Confederacy where such an institution can be productive of more good, this being the terminus of the Spartanburg and Union Railroad; the point at which a very large proportion of the sick and wounded soldiers both of this District and Northwestern North Carolina are delivered, unless they are cared for in this way, they must suffer."[35] The newspaper announced a concert to raise money for the Wayside Home.

The war meant death, not in the abstract but the death of relatives, close friends, and acquaintances. For most people living in the district who had sons, husbands, or friends in the army the war was a time of waiting. Knowing that death was always possible, indeed, probable as the years passed and the lists of dead grew longer, they could do nothing but wait. But for some citizens who could afford the time and money waiting was not enough. They traveled to their loved ones in the ranks. Meta Grimball, a refugee in Spartanburg from the low-country, recorded in her journal a pleasant conversation with Whitefoord Smith, the president of St. John's College where Mrs. Grimball was staying: "A clever, good, genial man, his only son is now with the Army, and he told us they had felt anxious to get warm clothes for him, and his wife a great contriver, had taken the checked flannel out of a large cloak of his and made some shirts for him. He bought a thick great coat, and intended going to Virginia to see his son and give him these warm clothes. The young man is just 18, and said he wished to take his share in this struggle and not have it said to him when the independence was achieved that he was enjoying what he had not worked for."[36] Two days later Mr. Smith received word that his son had been killed at the Battle of Manassas Junction. Smith never had to make his trip.

Built in the 1840s, the Walker House was the premier hotel in the village during the Civil War. Photograph courtesy of the Herald-Journal Willis Collection, Spartanburg County Public Libraries.

Others were much luckier. When Mrs. Walker, who ran the Walker House (a Spartanburg hotel), heard that her son had been killed in Virginia she set off to bring his body home. Her friends tried to discourage her from such a long, lonely, and perhaps dangerous trip, but she was a strong-willed woman. She was elated to find her son alive, though severely wounded, and credited her care of him all the way home with saving his life.[37] Such was not an idle boast, for medical care in the ranks was minimal. Sanitary conditions and medical knowledge were inadequate to the tremendous task of caring for so many sick and wounded. Such prompt attention from a loving parent could mean the difference between life and death. Other parents who traveled north to the battles did bring home dead sons. E. P. Smith went to Richmond to pick up the body of his son, Ralph, and while there visited with two other of his boys. He was appalled at the death around him. Writing on the day after the battle of Malvern Hill, in which the Confederate forces lost over five thousand men in an almost suicidal attack on entrenched Union forces, Smith was anguished: "it is awful. I see thousands. Some killed others wounded. Auran Williams is killed. Samey McCravy, Capt. Lemp and John Gentry and thousands of others. John Rantree, Capel, Stribling and many others that you know."[38]

The letters, diaries, and journals of Spartanburg people kept during the war years record and comment on the deaths of friends and acquaintances during the first years of the war, but in the last two years little reference is made to death. Possibly it had become too commonplace to deserve special mention. For some in the village an army death had special poignancy, and perhaps because of social convention had to be borne in solitude. Meta Grimball mentions a young lady who "seems broken hearted. She has been engaged 3 years to Mr. Palmer . . . the 3 young men, Whiteford Smith, [T. L.] Capers & [J. J.] Palmer were in the Spartan Rifles and shot by one ball [killed by the same shell] & found lying close together. It would have been a comfort to this poor girl if she had been married to her love, and then she could have mourned with his family and had a claim on their sympathy."[39]

Men who left their families to go to war, or worse were killed, most often left their loved ones in a destitute condition. Seventy percent of the heads of households in 1860 in Spartanburg District did not own slaves, and about half of the heads of households did not even own their own land. So when the man left, the bread earner in the family was gone, and the family lost its major means of support. This problem became acute early in the war, especially when soldiers were irregularly paid their eleven dollars a month. In addition, the rampant inflation which had quickly affected Confederate currency further reduced even that little money in value. In view of such difficulties, district politicians gave a high priority to obtaining some relief for the families of soldiers.

In 1862 South Carolina's legislature authorized district boards to raise a new local tax for soldiers' relief. The upper districts, and especially Spartanburg, benefitted little from what proved to be a discriminatory legislation. Spartanburg had a large white population but was a poor district with relatively few slaves. Not many Spartanburg District residents could claim exemption by virtue of owning twenty or more slaves, so the district had a large proportion of its white population in the ranks. Therefore, any tax which could substantially aid soldiers' families had to be heavy and would fall on a small number of taxpayers. On the other hand, because so many lowcountry planters owned over twenty slaves the proportion of lowcountry men in the ranks was much smaller than in the upper districts. Consequently, the total support needed for soldiers' families in the Lowcountry was smaller than in the upper districts and could be spread over many more taxpayers.[40] As state politicians haggled over what form relief should take, the price of provisions in the upper districts continued to climb rapidly. The situation got so bad that the executive committee of the state revoked all permits in the area to distill grains in spite of the medicinal needs of soldiers. Finally, in December of 1862, under extreme pressure from these same districts, the legislature took $600,000 from the state treasury and appropriated it to districts according to the proportion of the white population for the relief of soldiers' families.[41]

Finally the legislature recognized the collective responsibility of the state for these destitute people. Yet, given the degree of need, that money did not go very far, and the districts were soon once again dependent on their own resources. In December 1863, after the discouraging defeats of that summer and fall (Vicksburg, Gettysburg, and Chattanooga) the legislature assessed a tax in kind of 2 percent on food and 5 percent on manufactured goods produced for public sale to be paid to the relief boards. In 1864 the tax on food rose to 3 percent in order to provide every eligible family five bushels of grain. The legislature required districts to share the proceeds of the tax after their own needs were met. The tax in kind was unpopular in Spartanburg District and officials had difficulty in collecting it.[42] The three district officials responsible for collecting the tax finally resorted to threats published in the *Spartan:* "TAX IN KIND When the Farmer or Planter, shall fail to deliver his Taxes in Kind as required by law, he is required to pay five times the estimated value of the portion not delivered, to be collected in the manner according to the Act provided. As many persons in this District have failed to return their Tax in Kind, or to report thereon and many who have not signed their original report to assessors, notice is hereby given, on failure to [do] so early, the law will be rigorously enforced against them. T. O. P. Vernon J. B. Cleveland J. M. Elford."[43]

Complaints from destitute district residents abounded. One B. Bonner was driven by his inability to fulfill the needs of the district's soldier families to have the *Spartan* publish the following:

> Notice[:] At the last session of the Legislature, I was appointed of the Commissioners for Spartanburg District, for the soldier's families, very much against my wish. My experience has been very limited; not having had an opportunity to meet with the Board, who could have instructed me. With the means afforded me, I have done the best I knew how. Still I hear rumors afloat that I have not done right. Now if any respectable man will come and examine my transactions and will say, after examination, that any Soldier's wife in my beat has on my account suffered loss in money matters, I will restore unto her double.[44]

The people of Spartanburg District were not used to paying taxes, and their reluctance to do so illustrated a major problem for the nascent Confederacy—the reluctance of Southerners to think in terms of the needs of the community, much less the whole nation. Individualism, with its meaning of self-reliance, ran strong in Southern blood.

3

Spartanburg Beleaguered

Many residents of Spartanburg accepted the privations of war because they believed they were fighting for the right. But except for the initial year of fighting and the spring of 1863, when it seemed Vicksburg would withstand federal onslaught and General Robert E. Lee was invading the North, the war was depressing. After 1863, when Vicksburg was lost, General Lee repulsed at Gettysburg, and General Braxton Bragg embarrassed at Chattanooga, people feared a bad end might be inevitable and, depending on a loss of morale in the Union, their best efforts futile.

Together, the blockade of Southern ports, the state bans on the export of cotton, and the constant demands of war which exceeded the South's industrial capacity created unprecedented economic hardship throughout the Confederacy. The Confederate Congress urged producers not to take cotton to market "for fear the Lincolnites will steal it," and several states banned its export in the hope that such a loss to the European textile industry would force France and England to recognize the legitimacy of the Confederate government. Many Spartanburg farmers who were off to war left orders with overseers not to plant the crop if the blockade was not lifted because "should the blockade continue, it will be [a] useless waster of labor to raise another crop."[1] More and more Spartanburg farmers came to depend on cotton as a money crop during the 1850s. Even owners of relatively small acreage came to grow a bale or two, which lifted them out of the ranks of subsistence farmers by providing some spending money. The drop in production after 1860 resulted in a drastic reduction of their incomes.

Even more troublesome was the war's drain on the district's manpower. Spartanburg District had relatively few persons who were exempted from military service and many of its farmers had to go to war. An amateur historian at the end of the nineteenth century went to considerable trouble to gather the names of all of the men from Spartanburg who had served in the armed forces of the

Confederacy. He estimated that from three to four thousand men served in the Confederate Service, South Carolina Militia, State Reserves, or Cadet Corps.[2] Spartanburg men served in about thirty-three different companies, two regiments of which were largely manned by soldiers from the district. This amounted to 40 percent or more of eligible white men from Spartanburg District in service.[3] As soldiers abandoned farms, food crops became more scarce every year, and prices jumped. "Times are becoming scary" wrote one farmer in 1862, and he was not far off the mark.[4] In 1863, Jefferson Davis urged farmers, and especially planters, to turn from growing cotton to growing food; the army needed it, and the people needed it. The Carolina *Spartan* also urged a re-emphasis on growing provisions, for "there is much depending this year on our agricultural pursuits. Patriotism demands of us to go cheerfully into this work—the time has come when we are compelled to plant the cereals for our use—let every man do his duty now."[5]

The weather seemed especially unfavorable during some of the war years—people complained of it bitterly—and crops were poor. But more than anything else, in Spartanburg there just weren't enough men available to do the farming, and bad weather made a small crop even thinner. "I fear that starvation may conquer us sooner than the Yankeys" lamented one farmer with some hyperbole. Things were not quite that bad, but unusually heavy rains in the spring of 1862 and again in 1863 made for exceptionally low yields. The farmers were despondent and David Harris claimed "to be conqu[ered] over. There is nothing to boast of in the way of good crops. Our mellons . . . from our garden is not good. The wheat & oats are nearly ruined and corn is late & low. Corn is coming into demand at this time [July]. All are enquiring who has to sell."[6] The lament was justified; in 1862 he had made only twenty-five of the 250 bushels of wheat he expected, and 1863 did not turn out any better. Farmers struggled to grow enough food to feed themselves and had little prospect of having any grain to sell. Some farmers, having more acreage than they could tend with available manpower and under bad weather conditions, began to rent out their land for the first time. They would have preferred not to rent, but it was a way to make some badly needed money: suddenly everything was selling for cash at inflated prices.

Provisions were scarce, but enough food was available to prevent starvation—at a price. Salt was the only food item that had to be imported into the district. People used salt to preserve meat, and the need for it was so acute that farmers and villagers put together wagon trains and sent them to Richmond to buy it. They returned with disappointingly little salt and had to pay from thirty to sixty dollars a bushel for what they got.[7] There were some local farmers who managed to get their hands on salt and they took advantage of their good fortune by advertising in the *Spartan:* "Notice. I will exchange SALT, pound for pound, for gross pork; also, exchange salt for any of the products of the country, selling Salt at the smallest rates, and allowing the highest prices for the prodducts."[8]

So it went for all farm goods. The laws of supply and demand and cheap money all worked their inevitable result. The price of corn, the mainstay of a Southerner's diet, provides an example of what hard times could do. In 1859 in Spartanburg District corn was selling for about fifty cents ($13.50) a bushel, in 1862 it sold for one dollar ($22.40), in 1863 it sold for $3.25 ($58.20), in 1864 it sold for ten dollars ($143), and at the end of the war, in April 1865, it was selling for twenty dollars ($276) a bushel.[9]

Farmers could raise some corn and hogs for themselves, and if there was a little left over to sell, the village dwellers had to pay premium prices for it. In this, as in other emergencies, the wealthy had a decided advantage, and everybody knew it. Inflation's effect was not limited to food items; during the war the price of all necessities rose, especially the cost of yarn. By the spring of 1864 villagers were paying as much as fifteen dollars ($215) a yard for flannel and two dollars ($28.60) a spool for cotton. Shoes were in demand for the army—legion are the stories of shoeless Confederates—and leather was almost impossible to obtain. Shoes, if they could be had at all, were costing seventy-five dollars ($1,070) a pair in 1864. At that price very few people could purchase them, and many persons taught themselves the art of shoe repairing. Luxury items were almost totally out of the question. The laws prohibiting the making of spirits from grains did not wholly shut the industry down, but it severely decreased the supply. On November 13, 1862, the *Spartan* published a resolution: "A public meeting after the end of the session of court resulted in the following proclamation: 'whereas, the distillation of grain into spirits is threatening the most serious consequences to the country and whereas the Governor and Executive Council have issued their proclamation invoking all licenses to distill grain from and after the 10th day of this month therefore Resolved That the people of Spartanburg District here assembled express their hearty concurrence in the action of the Executive authority, and pledge their support to the said action by every means in their power.'" In spite of this resolution spirituous liquors remained available, and fruit became an increasingly valuable item—a gallon of brandy cost fifty dollars ($896) in 1863.

High prices and bad weather were not the only trials which plagued farmers. By 1862 farmers were complaining about taxes. This was especially true of creditors who the state legislature prevented from collecting debts with a stay law. There were local taxes raised for the relief of soldiers' families as well as Confederate taxes in specie and in kind. Although tax collection was slow, most people would have agreed with David Harris who believed "our taxes are heavy, but we must submit to it without a murmur, for money must be had to carry on the war."[10] Perhaps another reason why people were willing to pay their taxes is that by the summer of 1863 there was more Confederate money around but "people do not fancy it much . . . [and are] anxious to get rid of it." With the removal of the stay law debtors rushed to pay their debts with this highly inflated currency, but creditors would have none of it. After 1863, the real attitude of many people toward the Confederacy is probably best measured by their reluctance to accept its money. In February of 1865 Emily Harris "went to Ben Finch's to try to pay off a note. I could not do it. He would have nothing I've got, Creditors once were glad to be paid. Now they flee from a settlement as from a pestilence. Confederate money is trash."[11]

Under wartime conditions some inflation was to be expected, but many residents of the district believed that several people were taking advantage of the basic needs of their neighbors. To a few persons this was good business, to others it was speculation, and to even more it amounted to extortion. The *Carolina Spartan* made clear its position:

> EXTORTION and SPECULATION Upon this subject a great deal has been written, with how little effect, the multiplication of the disease, socially and morally, clearly shows. . . . numerous persons who we esteemed as above its influence have been ensnared and subdued to its power. . . . it appears at one time in the article of corn, at another in the form of jeans, at another in the shape of merchandise, at another it assumes the liquidity of the peach and apple, rye and other cereals. . . . As soon as the distiller raises the price of corn . . . is the hue and cry raised that it be stopped. . . . Yet the tanner, the seller of wares and merchandise, the manufacturer of cloth and jeans are all permitted to bleed the heart, and empty the purse . . . and not one word of complaint is uttered by those who style themselves custodians of good morals and tender humanity. . . . An evil is an evil no matter who practices it. Stop them all if possible.[12]

The paper was articulating the unspoken feelings of many in the district whose lives were made difficult by high prices and scarcity. The desire for profit was proving stronger than patriotism among some who could find a way to exercise it. Two years later, however, the *Spartan* defended the manufacturers in the district from what it considered misplaced criticism: "Manufacturers[:] This much abused class it seems are entitled to more credit for patriotic acts that is usually accorded them. We are informed by an officer whose business it is to know such things, that within the last month Bivingsville Factory has furnished the Government with 8,000 or 10,000 pounds of bacon, 1,000 sacks and 90 bunches yarn, to be exchanged for bacon. Hill's Factory has also furnished 5,000 pounds of bacon. This is aid and comfort in the right direction. We record them with pleasure, and hope that other manufacturing establishments will share with them in the munificence of their aid to the government."[13]

The scarcity of cloth was an especially bad problem. The Bivingsville mill had committed most of its cloth to the military and could only sell a small portion of its output locally. Because of the limited quantity of yarn available and the depreciation of currency the price rose rapidly. Unlike other establishments, the Bivingsville plant continued to accept Confederate money very late into the war, but that willingness did little to blunt popular resentment aimed at the owner of the mill, John E. Bomar, and his superintendent, Dexter E. Converse. The Carolina *Spartan* defended the businessmen as loyal patriots who were doing the best that could be done under trying conditions:

> While many misanthropic and unpatriotic proprietors of Factories are demanding gold or silver for their yarn, Confederate money is quite current at Bivingsville; nor are the prices beyond the advance made in all other kinds of merchandize. . . . It is unjust to criminate these gentlemen, as some foolishly do, for the high prices, or because they cannot furnish each individual with an indefinite amount of yarn, as these circumstances are entirely beyond their control. Would that all the complainers, whiners and croakers of the land were doing as much for the material benefit of our country, and the comfort of our people, as the proprietors and managers of this establishment.[14]

The policy of the mill was to sell the available yarn at the factory door in quantities limited per customer, but to the highest bidder. Bidding angered the small farmer by cutting him out of the market, and those persons who could afford to bid were unhappy at being limited to the purchase of one bunch of yarn. The crowds that gathered at the mill for the bidding pushed, shoved, cursed, begged, and even prayed for yarn. The management of the mill invited public scorn because they abused the practice of limiting sales by allowing some people to purchase relatively large quantities.

David Harris was one of these people. At first he bought only for his personal use, but soon he came to realize the profits that could be made from speculating in yarn. In the fall of 1862, he began by buying bunches of thread and weaving jeans which he sold for a profit of over one hundred dollars ($2,240). By the spring of 1863 he and Emily were "talking of making a large lot of cloth for sale. I do not like to be called a speculater, but I want to make some thing to live upon."[15] After purchasing twenty-five bunches of yarn David walked all over his neighborhood, trying to hire local women to weave it into cloth. Soon he was trading some of his land, which under different circumstances he was loathe to sell, for large quantities of cotton which he later sold for yarn. In April he bought forty-five bunches of yarn at six dollars ($134) each. He sold part of them in May at ten dollars ($224) each and the rest in June for $12.50 ($280). He continued to speculate as long as the goods were available and the transactions profitable. By 1864 wartime conditions forced the Bivingsville Mill to announce in the *Spartan:* "Cotton Yarn. Notice is hereby given to the public, that for the next three months to come we *cannot* dispose of Cotton Yarn for money, in consequence of having to supply the Government with a large proportion of what we manufacture. WE CAN ONLY EXCHANGE FOR PROVISIONS. NONE OTHER NEED APPLY. JOHN BOMAR & CO. Bivingsville, June 16, 1864."[16] Even manufacturers who six months earlier had been praised by the *Spartan* for their patriotism had, at last, come to grips with the worthlessness of Confederate money. Patriotism had lost its luster to cruel reality.

E. P. Smith, meanwhile, was being urged by his son Eliphas not to miss out on the demand for brandy. The Smiths owned large groves of fruit trees and Eliphas believed "you should try and make as much money out of yours as you can." It was possible for Elihu to make four or five hundred gallons which were worth about forty dollars ($717) each in 1863 with the prospect of that price doubling in a few months.[17]

Farm people fared better during the hard times of war than village people did. At the very least farmers could grow food and had time to provide themselves with homemade goods, and demand created opportunities for those who were substantial farmers. People like Smith could sell their pork at very high prices, and with the demand for any meat so great, even Smith's herd of relatively poor cows could be sold for a fine profit. Whenever David Harris started off to the village with meat to sell someone along the road almost always bought it for prices that astounded even him. Bacon prices were so good, for instance, that Harris stopped eating it himself; he switched his family to beef so he could sell the hogs. But after late 1863 such speculation became very risky. The declining worth of currency made accepting cash too uncertain, so individuals took a cue from John Bomar's Bivingsville Mill and ceased accepting Confederate currency for much of anything at all. Most people who had anything to speculate with turned to barter which made the entire process cumbersome and far less profitable.

In addition to the problems of declining food, inflation, and an increasingly worthless money supply, the people of Spartanburg District had to contend with a breakdown in law and order. Although they had traditionally preferred to settle disputes personally and without reference to constituted authorities, there had always been circumstances where they had had to resort to their judicial system. During the war, probably because of the decrease of manpower, the judicial system seems to have deteriorated. Although the Magistrates' and Freeholders'

Court continued to function seemingly well (many white people wanted to keep a tight lid on their slaves and free negroes) other parts of the court system suffered.[18] In 1861, Benjamin Finch, a neighbor of David Harris, shot and killed Dr. G. H. King. At first David Harris was called as a character witness for Finch, but after several delays in the Finch trial, Harris was added to the jury. Harris had made several trips to Spartanburg village for this trial only to find that in every instance the trial had been postponed (for a fuller discussion of this bizarre case see Chapter Seven). The trial would not actually take place until 1866, well after the war ended. In 1861, the first time that the Finch trial was set to begin, Harris recorded in his diary an account of another trial that same day in which a man had been found guilty and hanged. So in 1861, as the war had just begun, trials were taking place, but as the war wore on larger numbers of men from the District were called to render military service. Harris made his subsequent trips to the village only to find that there was no court at all.[19]

Also, as the numbers of soldiers who were coming through the district on their way home increased—some had legitimately left their units and some were deserters—people in the district became apprehensive. Foodstuffs began to disappear; livestock was found butchered in the field. Some people in the district believed this was the work of these soldiers or deserters. Others believed it the work of slaves, but in either case the situation was growing more worrisome. In addition, increasing numbers of travelers began showing up on doorsteps asking for food or shelter. Farm women whose husbands were still in service were warned by their neighbors not to grant shelter to the men who sought it.[20]

Except for the first two years when the Confederacy seemed triumphant on the field of battle, the war had a depressing and ominous fatality about it. The Confederacy expected to wear down the Union by making the war so deadly and costly that the North would choose to give up the contest rather than make the enormous sacrifice necessary for victory. It was not victory which the South sought but terms giving it independence. The strategy depended on a superior willingness among Confederates to resiliently make sacrifices. Through 1862 it appeared as if the South might achieve its aims as the North met reverses and the South parried blow after blow. Generally, the poor performance of Northern armies seemed to indicate a decided Southern advantage in military leadership which assured the outcome. But such assumptions proved unwarranted.

The reaction of people in Spartanburg District to the changing fortunes of war are reflected in the journals of David Harris. Here are recorded the reactions of an intelligent and discriminating owner of a middle-sized farm to the progress of the war. Because of his wide circle of friends and the social and political connections which he enjoyed through his father's position in the village—his father was the owner of over fifty slaves, a leader of the First Baptist Church, and a founder of the first of Spartanburg's schools—it seems likely that David and his wife Emily reflected the views of at least part of the district's leadership class and general population. Although David owned slaves, most of his immediate neighbors did not. Unlike some people in Spartanburg David was not given to bombast, nor was he easily taken in. He was not beyond making profit from war conditions, but in order to do so he had to be a keen and realistic observer of his surroundings. By March of 1862, after some initial Confederate victories but before the major battles had been fought, David was uneasy but determined: "The war is assumeing a rather ugly appearance. The people are becoming alarmed. I think that war is not the game of fun that they did at the commencement. But now is the time for patriots to show their vaunted patriotism. When it is most needed, I fear it will be the hardest to find. Now that we have put our hands to the plow, and our necks are in the haulter. We must not look back; nor dispond, but strain ever more to accomplish our independence."[21]

In the next few months many Southerners were anxious as battles loomed but, in general, the news was good. Although New Orleans was lost in May, Shiloh had been won in April and McClellan repulsed before Richmond in late June. A reverse for Lee at Sharpsburg in September was offset by his saving his army. It seemed that the South's strategy of an essentially defensive position would wear

Dead Confederates after the Battle of Antietam. Courtesy of the Library of Congress. Prints and Photographs Division.

the Union down. After all, the Confederacy was a huge territory which the Union army had to conquer and occupy. The Confederate government counted on the daunting nature of that task.

1863 proved to be a different matter. In the fall of 1862 and the spring of 1863 the South achieved her greatest victories. In December 1862 the federals were again repulsed before Richmond at Fredericksburg and then again in May 1863 at Chancellorsville. But the wages of war are fickle, and some two months later, in July 1863 after Confederate defeats at Gettysburg and Vicksburg, things looked bleak. David Harris recorded the picture:

> How tired some of us are getting of the war. I am tired of asking for, & hearing the news. At this time everything wears a gloomy aspect. Our army that was in Pensyvania [Pennsylvania] have recrossed the Potomac. Having accomplished but little, but lost thousands of men. Vicksburg have fallen, and our armyes in the West are retreating. The Mississippi is in the control of the Yankees. Charleston is beseiged and will probable fall. Then we will certainly see, feel, & taste what we have so far escaped but if it must be it will be. So we must make the best we can of it. As for me, I am far from saying that we are conquered, or will be conquored so long as our men are united. I can see nothing so desperate but that it could be much worse. And nothing so bad, but that it may be redeemed. So we must put our trust in providence & fight on.[22]

The catalogue was depressing, but the determination and the faith indicated here were just as real. Lee had saved his army at Gettysburg, and if places such as Vicksburg were lost, Southern armies were not being destroyed. The succession of reverses, however, did give opponents of the incumbent national, state, and local governments an opportunity for exploitation, and the political opposition in Spartanburg District was quick to take advantage of it.

The fall of 1863 was the time for the second congressional election. In 1861, James Farrow had easily been elected from the fifth district which included Spartanburg. Farrow was vehemently opposed for re-election by Dr. John Winsmith who supported the candidacy of the Rev. James P. Boyce. Farrow's opponents attacked him as being inept and doing nothing for the district. In a letter to the *Spartan,* "Leonidas Spartan" defended the incumbent and attacked Boyce's supporters by claiming that "we need no oracular responses now to inform us who are the friends and who the enemies of our cause. The man who predicts the downfall; nay? Proclaims the *death* of the Confederacy, that he may dig up treasures for himself out of its mammoth grave—is he its friend?"[23] Farrow's opposition tried hard to make an issue of his support for hard and necessary war measures, and his supporters, in turn, worked to make criticism of the government tantamount to treason: "It is treason now to despair of the Confederacy, or utter a sentiment unfavorable to our final and speedy triumph. The cause is God's and it must prevail."[24]

There was a general reaction against the government of Jefferson Davis in the Congressional elections which ran from June to November, and opponents of the government were widely elected.[25] Yet in the fifth district, general confidence continued to rest with Farrow. He defeated the Rev. Mr. Boyce by 1145 votes out of 4375 cast. In Spartanburg District Farrow's opponents were badly divided. Dr. Winsmith's brother, Elihu, supported Farrow because he considered Boyce an inept demagogue. Except for Dr. Winsmith and his supporters, most residents of the District were not so much angry at what they considered the government's failures, as they were uneasy with, but resigned to, the sacrifices war made necessary.[26] In the fall of 1863, Jefferson Davis was pushing the Confederate Congress to impose still higher taxes, both pecuniary and in kind, enroll even more men into the ranks of draftees, and in general demand more of these sacrifices of the Confederacy's citizens. Legislation to these ends passed the Confederate Congress by the end of the year.

By December 1863 David Harris could see the war was going from bad to worse. "If any one should raise the veil of futurity and ask me to look I should not have courage to do it," he wrote as he began to despair. He seemed to know the inevitable loss his section would suffer and worried about what to do to prepare for it. He wondered whether to sell all he could for fear it would be worth nothing later or to keep all, sell nothing, and hope times would make his goods valuable once again. It was, indeed, a bad sign for the Confederacy when someone like David Harris could bring himself to comment on business matters: "I suppose . . . it makes but little difference anyway." By the spring of 1864 he decided to pull his children out of school and put them to work in the fields—he needed bread for next year.[27] This was an extremely difficult decision for David and Emily Harris. They both firmly believed in the necessity of educating their children, including their girls, and they both devoted much time, energy, and resources to the education of their family. Finally, by 1865, the Harrises were convinced the war was lost.

It was left for the last desperate, almost ludicrous, and feeble efforts of the Civil War in South Carolina to be played out in Spartanburg District. When the Union army commanded by General William T. Sherman approached Columbia, the Governor of South Carolina, Andrew G. Magrath, fled to Spartanburg. Magrath wrote to several military men offering to put together a force "adequate to any emergency likely to arise;" his gesture was aimed primarily at putting down renegades and raiders who infested the upper districts. It was an empty gesture as there were no troops with which to create a "force" of any kind.[28] The desperation evident in Magrath's hollow offer was shared by Spartanburg's residents.

As the war effort broke down, soldiers straggled back to Spartanburg or passed through on their way home. These men had not been paid in months. Even those who had money found that it was of no value. Confederate money was useless by March of 1865. Soldiers, many of whom had remained more enthusiastic about the war longer than the people back home and who had suffered so many hardships for the war effort, became enraged when their pitifully few dollars were refused as payment for any goods. Driven by anger, hunger, and desperation some struggling soldiers became a mob and took what they were not allowed to buy. One store owner in the village of Spartanburg "incurred their ill will by refuseing Confederate money for groceries & they made a rade [raid] upon his Store House & robbed it of about five thousand dollars worth of goods."[29]

Finally in April of 1865 the war actually came to Spartanburg for a brief moment. Federal troops chasing Jefferson Davis stopped in Spartanburg. William Kennedy Blake, the president of the Spartanburg Female College, gives a vivid recollection of the incident:

Shorly after my return I was called to the door one Sunday morning just after breakfast and saw near the steps a man on horse back, wearing a broadbrimmed slouch hat and his body covered with an oilcloth. He told me that he was on his way to the army and wished to get some information with regard to the roads. I asked him to dismount and to come into the house, but he declined, saying that his party was waiting for him. It was such a common thing to have soldiers to call going to or returning from the army that at first I thought but little of the incident. I was impressed however, by the intelligence of the man and tact he displayed in seeking the information he desired. After learning the principal roads which led out of Spartanburg and the names of some of the prominent men in the vicinity, he very politely thanked me and bade me good-morning. I thought no more of the matter until about two oclock in the afternoon: At the usual hour in the morning I had accompanied the girls to church in the village: After dining at about one oclock I went to my sitting room and was resting upon the sofa: While lying there half asleep, Willie, who was about three years old, ran into the room, and jumping up and down, as if he had something good to tell, said "Papa, Papa, the Yankees are coming!" The servants who were near the Chapin house looking at the Yankees as they entered the town on Church Street, told Willie to go and tell me. At first I scarcely noticed him, but as he repeated that the Yankees were coming and seemed to be so full of it, I got up and went to the door and then to the street. Sure enough I saw the cavalry filing down Church Street! I know there was no time to be lost if I would save three fine horses I had in the stable. I called Claude Smith, my nephew, and Mr. Alderman, who was a professor in the college, and, bridling the horses as quickly as possible Alderman mounted one and Claude another, leading the third. I gave Claude directions where to take them and to remain with them until I came to him. The place selected was a swamp about 15 miles from the college and near Dick Cole's house. In the meantime I had given instructions to the girls not to leave their rooms and to conceal their money and valuables upon their persons. Before Alderman returned a party of half a dozen Yankees, went to my stable to secure my horses, but finding the stalls empty, they came to the house in front of which I was standing: they first asked me where my horses were: I replied that they were somewhere between Spartanburg and Greenville, but as they were making very good speed when I last saw them, I supposed by that time they had covered considerable distance. They left me and galloped toward the village. Hearing that the general in command had made his head-quarters at Mr. Bobo's residence, I got several friends to remain on the campus while I went at once to see the General and ask for protection for the college and the girls under my care. My request for an interview being granted, I was surprised and yet pleased to see in the officer before me the man who had been on the campus that morning asking about the roads: I made known to him the responsible position I occupied and the exposed condition of the college, and appealed to him as a soldier and a parent to give me all necessary protection. He treated me with the utmost courtesy and assured me that I should have ample protection and that he would punish severely any interference with the persons or property of the college by his soldiers. Thanking him I retired, after receiving from him the assurance that a guard would be detailed to remain at the college during his stay in Spartanburg. It was well that this precaution was taken, for in several instances straggling parties came on the campus and evidently intended mischief, but were driven off by the guard. The party that was after my horses in the afternoon came again at night thinking perhaps I had brought them in, but they were mistaken, though they swore that they would have them before they left. After night I took a bag of corn on my shoulder for the horses and some provisions for Claude and started for the swamp: I was afraid to trust any of the negroes with the corn lest they might disclose the hiding place to the Yankees. Not a single person on the campus except myself know the spot, not even Mr. Alderman, for I found afterwards that he had got separated from Claude and had dismounted and hitched the horse he had in charge to a tree and returned to the college. The first intimation of this fact was made known to me while on my way to Claud: Hearing the whinney of a horse a short distance from my path, I turned aside to reconnoiter, not knowing but that some Yankee might be in hiding. Concealing my corn and provisions I crept noiselessly towards the place from which the whinney had come: When I got near the spot I heard another whinney, and waiting and listening awhile, I advanced a little further, and there, tied to the tree and alone I found the horse that Alderman had ridden from the campus. Without delay I threw the sack of corn on his back, and mounting him, was soon with Claud in the swamp. I found the horses all safe and that Claud had carried out my instructions to the letter. I went to Dick Cole's house and made arrangements for Claud to eat and sleep there until I should notify him that it was safe to bring the horses in. I returned to the college and remained on watch during the night, quieting the girls and patrolling the premises. Early the next morning the rascals were again at the stable in search of my horses, for they had doubtless been told of their value and were itching to get hold of them: A great many of the citizens lost their horses and some of them had their watches taken from them on the street, while in some instances valuables were taken from dwellings. They stole Dr. Shipps horse but when the Gen. was informed of it he ordered that another be sent to him. At this time there lived in Spartanburg a family of refugees from Charleston by the name of Hugenon: the daughter, Miss Ella H- was quite a fast young lady and possessed of no little self-assertion: while the Yankees were in line in front of her home she went to the gate and waved a Confederate flag in their faces! She was ordered to put it down, which she refused to do: The officer then snatched it from her, and, as she said, struck her in the face with it: She went immediately to head-quarters and reported the officer to the Gen. After hearing her statement the Gen. replied—"I am sorry Miss, that your conduct merited all that you received and I can do nothing for you." Miss H- turned upon him and said: "I am not surprised at the infamous conduct of your men when they have for a leader one who is destitute of every instinct of a gentleman!" The Gen. then ordered her from his presence. Those who witnessed the interview expected every moment to hear an order issued for her arrest, and were surprised at the General's leniency. Miss H- during the entire interview, did not seem to be the least intimidated and was defiant to the last.

On the morning of the third day the Yankees left town, going south, and by noon the last straggler had disappeared. To my surprise however, about dusk, those rascals who seemed bent on getting my horses returned and were seen prowling about the stables. The night passed and no more was seen or heard of them: as a matter of precaution however, I kept my horses several days longer in the swamp and had the satisfaction of thwarting the designs of these thieving rascals and of saving all three of my horses. Quite a number of young negro men followed the Yankees and never returned to Spartanburg.[30]

The white inhabitants of Spartanburg now felt the despair of defeat. Although much of everyday life had continued during the conflict as it always had, most of its dimensions had felt the impact of devastating war. Although Spartanburg had not endured physical destruction, it certainly had felt institutional strain. One of the institutions fundamental to the construction of its society, slavery, had been destroyed by the conflict. Fully one third of the district's population were slaves at the beginning of 1865 and were free persons by the end of April of that year. Now we turn our attention to the contours of slavery as it existed in Spartanburg District at the war's beginning and examine the impact of that conflict on the institution and the enslaved.

4

Slavery during the War

Slavery had existed in Spartanburg from the time of the first settlements in the middle of the 18th century. By 1860 the district's total population was about twenty-eight thousand, and the village population was about one thousand to one thousand two hundred. About one third of the district's total population were slaves (there were about fifty free African Americans). Close to one-third of the white heads of households owned slaves. Close to one-half of the slave owners owned six or fewer slaves, and almost all owned under twenty slaves.[1]

During the war many Southerners, even in a small, relatively isolated village such as Spartanburg, worried about the behavior of their slaves. During the antebellum years Spartanburg's slave owners had been concerned about revolts. Although white people continued to be in total control of society, the strains of war made them increasingly anxious about how their slaves might react under changing circumstances—such as the absence of a male master and the deprivations of food and other items caused by the war. Apprehension about slave revolts continued unabated during the war.[2] Concerns about the activities of slaves grew from 1863 onward, as the news of the war became more dire. Slave owners worried about "negro-frolick[s]"; David Harris was asked to bring his gun and join a neighborhood posse to put an end to such a gathering. He decided to participate: "I went according to request (but without my gun) and *bravly* charged upon the house. But it was dark, silent & quiet, so we charged home again."[3] Obviously David had not taken this particular threat seriously. By 1864 and early 1865, when he was off in the lowcountry fighting for his country, his wife, Emily, began to have the same concerns as her neighbors. She came to share those worries not only because she had been left alone to manage her work force, but more important because she discovered some of her hogs butchered or stolen. She came to believe that "our hogs are killed for revenge as well as gain. We have insulted a negro who is too smart to be detected in his villainy." She found one of her slaves

African Americans picking cotton, the district's major staple crop. Photograph courtesy of the Herald-Journal Willis Collection, Spartanburg County Public Libraries.

stealing from her: "He steals and lies and disobeys all laws with the utmost impunity" and she learned that her slaves were harboring escaped Yankee prisoners. Finally she decided to whip one of her field hands. She grew afraid of her slaves as they became increasingly unruly, a result of their growing awareness that the end of the war meant their eventual freedom.[4]

There was reason for concern. Spartanburg's slaves had, for the most part, been docile and obedient during the antebellum period, but as the records of the Magistrates and Freeholders' Court demonstrate there were times when slaves lost control over themselves and acted contrary to expectations. These unexpected events had raised concerns over potential slave behaviors, which ranged from slaves openly flouting laws or traditional rules of conduct, to refusing to take or promptly obey orders, to violence toward white people.[5] The war caused those anxieties to become even more common. To make matters increasingly worse, the discovery of a plot (admittedly amorphous and perhaps apocryphal) for an insurrection in late 1859 and early 1860 had shaken at least the leaders of the community to a state of anxious watchfulness way beyond the norm of Spartanburg's antebellum past.[6]

The following reviews the normal functioning of Spartanburg's slave system during the antebellum years as people tried to control slave behavior and in turn slaves tried to establish lives of their own. The changes in the control and daily routine of the slave system caused by the war may be judged against this background. Having worried about slave revolts during peacetime, Spartanburg slave owners could not help but be concerned about what their slaves might do when society was under great strain.

Slavery was an integral part of the antebellum society of upstate South Carolina just as it was throughout the South. The everyday functioning of the institution did not change immediately, but as the war years passed, elements of the slave system, and the rest of society, did undergo profound alteration. In contrast to the 80 percent slave populations of many lowcountry districts, only about one-third of the population of Spartanburg District were slaves. Still, many white people in the district devoted considerable time and energy to regulating the institution.

To understand how slavery functioned as a normal part of antebellum life in the district, it is fundamental to keep in mind that although Spartanburg's white population often looked on slaves as chattel property, such as a farm animal or a farm tool, that property was of a very special kind. Slaves were human beings with emotions, actions, and reactions. Their masters and the authorities often interacted with them in ways that were normally not associated with property. Many slaves recognized their condition and considered it impossible to change it. They knew that white people controlled the power structure of the district. Resistance was ultimately futile. There were agricultural units in Spartanburg that were large and accommodated more than twenty slaves (for historians that number of slaves on a farm constitutes the designation of a plantation), but the vast majority of slaves in the district lived on farms with six or fewer African Americans.

On the plantations the larger number of slaves greatly increased the opportunity for communal organization and independence from the prying eyes of their owners. On smaller farms there might be far less independence and more working side by side with the owner. This situation is illustrated in references in letters and journals to "white and black families." Letters written by white people who were away from the farm often include, "Say howdy to the Servants." White Southerners tended to refer to their slaves using the term "servants" and almost never used the word "slave." What reads like paternalism is misleading, however, for the relationship between slave and master was fundamentally one of power. The white owner had absolute control over his or her property, and at any moment harsh treatment, most likely in the form of a whipping, could ensue. In these situations the slaves had no recourse but submission.

Since slaves were subject to the foibles and issues of all humans, white people often sought to control the behavior of slaves as well as their labor. Laws aimed at controlling slaves ultimately also controlled slave owners. Those laws, in effect, told owners how to manage their slaves and restricted how they treated this particular type of property. Slave owners did not like being told what they could or could not do with their property. Records of their behavior indicate that they largely ignored the laws, be they state or local, pertaining to slave control. It appears that they believed that what they did on their own farms and plantations was nobody's business but their own.

During the antebellum years, some district leaders worried about fraternization, particularly in the village, between slaves and lower-class white people, and especially when such interaction involved liquor. In 1834 the state legislature had prohibited gaming and gambling between whites and blacks. Spartanburg's city council was even more concerned with the impact of alcohol on slaves. The village council members made tavernkeepers swear not to "sell give exchange barter or in any otherwise deliver any spirituous liquor to any slave or Slaves."[7] Such efforts proved ineffective, for on the whole, white people who were most affected by such ordinances ignored those laws. Their own self-interest superseded what the village and county leadership considered the good of the community. Even more aggravating to district leaders was the knowledge that some slaves distilled liquor and sold it to other slaves or, even worse, to white men. For violation of the ordinance prohibiting those practices the city council legislated a sentence of forty lashes for each infraction.[8] Yet the laws seemed to have no effect. In frustration the council tried to bribe slaves by offering five dollars to any one who would inform on white people who sold them liquor. The attempted bribe went the way of all the other ordinances. Probably feeling annoyed at being ignored on the issue, the council ordered the constable to arrest black people who were drunk and publicly whip them with the village council members looking on.[9]

A temperance movement in the 1850s was further empowered by frustration over the noncompliance with liquor laws, causing the council to pass an ordinance closing all the bars. In 1857, three years after the temperance ordinance had passed, the *Carolina Spartan* reported: "The misconduct of many negroes in our midst calls for remedy. Gambling and drinking are becoming fearfully common. These things can be practiced with much facility in the absence of efficient patrolling. If this necessary duty cannot be more faithfully performed, we think it behoves Council to make provision for paid marshalls, who should be abroad at all hours."[10] The newspaper's comment got at the root of the matter. The negative consequences of trafficking in liquor were not important enough to anyone to end it. Even more disturbing was that those consequences actually had not seemed important enough to the majority of white people in the district to encourage them to take on the onerous duties of patrolling.

Another issue emerged from the widespread practice of hiring out slaves in various ways. Spartanburg village had seemed more concerned than outlying areas with controlling slaves. In the rural areas of the district slaves were widely separated, usually forming small families or communities on individual farms and the few plantations in the area. Slaves could be watched according to the desire of

Slave apartments in the village of Spartanburg. Photograph courtesy of the Herald-Journal Willis Collection, Spartanburg County Public Libraries.

the individual owner. Things were different in the village. There slaves regularly came into contact with other slaves, all manner of white men and women, and what few free black people lived or worked in the village. News could not be kept from them. Masters who owned more slaves than they needed often hired them out or allowed their slaves to hire themselves out, requiring a percentage of their wages in return. Some masters even allowed their slaves to live out on their own as long as they did not get into trouble and paid their master whatever was due.

By the 1850s many whites were convinced that this system was dangerous, even in the little village of Spartanburg. During the 1850s larger Southern cities passed laws to segregate white people from black people, to deprive slaves of work in some trades, and to break up the network of relationships that had built up among some black people. The possibility for slaves and free black people to exist in a world of their own, independent of control and supervision, could be seen as a danger to the slave system. Such independence, many white people had come to believe, posed a threat to their control.[11]

So Spartanburg council set out to constrict slave movement further. Slaves had always been required to have passes from their owners allowing them to be off their farms or plantations. In an effort to tighten restrictions, in 1853 the council required that passes be valid only for twenty-four hours and that they specify where the slave was to go.[12]

In the larger cities such as Charleston, there was an effort in the 1850s to deprive slaves of skilled jobs, as many whites believed slaves competed with them for work.[13] The *Carolina Spartan* reacted to such attempts: "We are sorry to observe that several of our State exchanges are arguing against the employment of slaves in mechanical pursuits. . . . Should the effort be successful to drive slaves out of such employments, the property of the master is reduced in value. Slave mechanics are more valuable than ordinary field hands. . . . The policy should be to strengthen the slave system . . . by widening, rather than contracting, the sphere of employment, and make it the interest of every man to hold slaves."[14] As it turned out, there was no serious effort in Spartanburg to deprive slaves of the income from "mechanical pursuits." But there were efforts to deprive slaves of what little independence they had gained because of their masters' reluctance to patrol regularly.

The village council continued to enact a series of laws aimed at restricting slaves' freedom of movement, but such laws proved useless. What seemed to gall some white people about hiring out practices was the sense of independence they imagined these practices induced in the slave population. In 1857 this white frustration was exemplified in the following extreme and bizarre town ordinance: "If any slave shall walk with a cane or stick, except the aged and decrepit and infirm, or if any Slave or slaves smoke a cigar or pipe in the street or other public highways on the Sabbath or other days the slave . . . shall receive for each and every offence twenty lashes."[15] As with all laws, it was inevitable that some should be broken eventually.

In the 1820s the state legislature established the Court of Magistrates and Freeholders to adjudicate all cases that involved African Americans. The Spartanburg Court of Magistrates and Freeholders functioned between 1824 and 1865. Although the vast majority of punishments of slaves continued to take place on plantations and farms, there were instances where a formal court was necessary. These included capital cases and cases where a slave had allegedly acted improperly toward a white person, and the aggrieved party believed that the slave's owner had not reprimanded the slave properly. In a case brought before a magistrate, that magistrate would select eight freeholders, usually from the neighborhood where the slave lived. The accused, his owner, or in rare cases his lawyer, would choose five freeholders from among the eight who would then act as judge and jury. The magistrate would act as the prosecutor. The judgment in the case could be appealed to the appellate court, although such appeals were rare.[16]

When cases came to the magistrates' court we might expect, given the racial assumptions of the time, that the slave's guilt was easily proved or perhaps automatically assumed. But that was not always the case, and this court found only slightly more than half of the accused guilty (for both free blacks and slaves about forty percent of the cases were dismissed). The court seems to have been careful in examining the evidence placed before it, and on the whole, willing to evaluate conflicting testimony. In all of the 278 guilty verdicts rendered over the entire course of the court's existence, the punishment was a whipping, except in six cases where the slaves were hanged and two cases where slaves were placed in solitary confinement on bread and water.[17]

A whipping seems to have been somewhere between fifteen and forty lashes.[18] The whip was commonly a four-foot-long strip of cowhide about two inches wide and a quarter inch thick. In most cases it was attached to a wooden handle. Whips such as those portrayed in movies were almost never used to punish slaves as they would inflict mortal wounds. Although there appear to be no records of how many lashes on average constituted a whipping on farms in Spartanburg, according to the Magistrates' and Freeholders' Court records 46 percent of the punishments were between fifteen and thirty lashes. It is likely that the punishments administered on farms were no more, as otherwise the punishment would have made the recipient unable to work for several days. Also, on small farms the relationship between slaves and owners might have been close and led to a mitigated punishment. There were, of course, much more severe whippings administered by the courts for what were considered major crimes. One hundred or more lashes were administered in 41 out of 278 guilty verdicts ruled over the court's existence.

Most slave owners owned six or fewer slaves, probably a family. Therein existed the ultimate quandary—wives and mothers, husbands and fathers, and children were expected not to interfere when a family member was being whipped. It is difficult to imagine the horror of a person watching her or his spouse being whipped, or of parents watching a child, and not being able to do anything about it or the difficulty faced by the parent in explaining to a child why he or she had not chosen to interfere in the punishment. Any interference would have only resulted in physical punishment for both parents instead of just one. At times people decided to act in spite of the consequences.

Having cursed his master for whipping a female servant, one slave, on seeing his master advancing on him with a stick, struck the man with a wooden bat in self-defense.[19] The slave's actions cost him three hundred lashes and three months in prison. Of course slaves knew the consequences of interfering with such actions, but for some resistance was more important than a raw and livid back.

In another case a father, exclaiming that "he would be damned if he would stand it," cut loose his little boy who was being whipped by his master. When the owner came after the boy, the enraged slave father exclaimed, "Yes God damn you come on. I am ready for you," and he was, for he hit the owner with an ax. Described by his master as "a good boy & a faithful servant except when under the influence of liquor," the father was hanged for his love and protectiveness. Previously only liquor could loosen this man's self-control, but in the cold sobriety of this instant an unacceptable horror had served to release his pent up rage.[20]

Slaves who had been hired out had to be careful in their relationships, for many people in the community, especially its leadership, were mindful of the possibility that hired out slaves might come to think of themselves or act as free men. One such hired out slave, a carpenter by trade, was accused of insulting a white man who refused to pay for work the slave had done. When the carpenter had the temerity to ask for payment, the white man picked up a cane to thrash him. The slave "picked up a rock and then caught . . . the white man with his left hand and then with his Right hand . . . did give him one severe blow over the head cutting a hole through his hat and also cutting his head." The slave then shouted that "he would not work with any such a damned rascal as he was."[21] The court sentenced the carpenter to fifteen lashes for insolence (an extremely low sentence for a slave who had bloodied a white man) but also saw to it that he was paid. In cases where slaves had obviously been cheated or badly mistreated the court usually tried to right the wrong. At the same time the court always had to administer some kind of punishment, no matter what the circumstances, to any slave who had struck a white person.

In the various court cases there is testimony about drunken masters mistreating their slaves (see the notorious case in Chapter Five). These comments illustrate one of the worst features of slavery. Having people at one's total control could be morally debilitating. Masters who were cruel by nature could indulge their cruelty on hapless servants and indulge the darker side of their characters. At any moment anger, frustration, or anxiety could flare up in violence. The urge to act out those feelings could become overwhelming. Power over others could make reasonable people lose all control. For the slaves, such a condition was fearsome. Many slave owners accepted the slave system as the natural order of things and did not think about it day to day. For the slaves, such acceptance would have been difficult. At any moment, for any reason, the slave owner could become a law unto himself. Slaves had no recourse. To resist was often to increase the violence and punishment; to submit meant humiliation and physical harm, but it usually meant survival.

Yet in spite of the danger, there was resistance both during the antebellum period and during the war. Slaves sometimes cursed and struck their masters, or attacked other white people who had tried to discipline or otherwise control them. Slaves who had been beaten or whipped one too many times might turn on their masters and beat them in turn. In such cases some white people were surprised and even hurt that an otherwise faithful servant should reward "good treatment" with physical violence. For instance, Polly Burgess told the court that she had always treated her slave, Violet, "very well" but when Polly ordered Violet "to go off about her own business or I would strike her" Violet talked back. Polly then "struck but the slave took the weapon out [of] her hand and knocked her down and struck her again" three times. Polly was astounded at the behavior of her slave. She told the court that she believed Violet "thought she was an equal." The court sentenced Violet to one hundred lashes and two weeks in jail for her temper (ironically depriving her mistress of her services while Violet recovered from her punishment).[22]

In the very few cases when slaves had murdered or accidentally killed their masters the court sentenced the accused slave to hang. When slaves physically attacked their masters but did not kill them the court's sentence was not hanging, but it was still harsh. The court sentenced one slave who had avoided a whipping by stabbing his master in the stomach to six hundred lashes (ordinarily a death sentence), two hundred immediately and 125 at later times until six hundred had been reached (this gave the slave's initial wounds time to heal before having to endure the second set of lashes). Afterward the magistrate sold the slave out of state.[23]

Most slaves constantly lived in a quandary—it was unnatural to expect someone to stand and let himself be knocked around. It is almost unthinkable that anyone would have let himself be killed. In 1858 James Turner accused Jane, the slave of Mrs. Hines, of attacking him and "inflicting seven wounds on his head and face." Mrs. Hines, with the corroboration of two witnesses, testified that Turner had struck Jane with a stick. When the slave held up a "pidgin" to ward off the blows he had struck it from her hand, and "she clenched, and then fell near the fire place. I saw them fall one near one fire dog and the other fell near the other fire place. He struck his head against the fire dog. . . . I never saw her [Jane, the slave] show the least disposition to strike him, she only shewd a disposition to keep from being hurt herself." The court may have believed the slave and her mistress, but the court was not willing to find the slave innocent. Jane, even though she acted in self defense, had been violent with a white person. The court gave her the relatively light sentence of fifty lashes.[24]

The preceding examples are unusual. During the antebellum years most slaves lived with the constraints and parameters placed on them. Slave owners dealt with their slaves and administered punishments in private on their farms and plantations. Most slaves never faced the situations just described, but those who did paid the price for reacting. Many slaves took vicarious pleasure in the others' resistance. It appears to have been common to resist slavery by helping runaways.

Indeed, in 1859, just prior to the outbreak of the Civil War, there were runaways living in caves where several branches of the Tyger River run together. The runaways who dug the caves were from Robert Otts's plantation. They provided the shelter of their caves to other runaways (the number is unclear) who passed through the area. They had a couple of guns, and a man who had sheltered with them testified that he had "Heard all the black ones talking about the negros being set free. Anderson [one of the runaway slaves who had dug the caves] told him two men were coming from the North and about thirty thousand men with him to set them free and he expected they would all have to fight and if he was obliged to fight he would do the best he could." This escaped slave also testified that another of the cave dwellers told him about the same thing. Whether or not this testimony was truthful, it was the case that those slaves who had dug the caves helped other runaways. When discovered, these cave dwellers also testified that a white man from Union was going to lead them in a rebellion against Union and Spartanburg. The court did not believe this testimony, concluding that there may have been talk of such an insurrection but that it was probably greatly exaggerated. However remote the possibility of such a plot, the discovery of the caves agitated the area. In the charged atmosphere of the late 1850s, any hint of such a possibility was bound to excite concern. The particular court that heard this case was made up of some of the most prominent slaveholders of the district, and cooler heads prevailed. The court found only the runaways who had dug the caves guilty and pronounced that they "be now taken out and [in the presence of the court] each have fifty lashes given them on their bare backs well laid on with a strap and then be set at liberty [and returned to their masters]."[25]

Worried by these events the city council ordered that all slaves away from their master's premises and not "in company with some white person over the age of ten years" be arrested and whipped, and prohibited any "Negro frolic happening in the town."[26] All in all, the power structure effectively barred African Americans from the streets. So many of Spartanburg's citizens were particularly concerned about the behavior of their slaves when war broke out in 1861. In addition to the *Carolina Spartan*'s rather hysterical warning about fifth column activities inciting the district's "blackamoors," the city council ordered that any African American found on the streets after nine o'clock without a pass be jailed overnight and flogged twenty lashes.[27]

The apprehension about the slave population is also reflected in articles in the *Carolina Spartan* such as the January 8, 1863, edition which reported: "On Christmas day some of the colored people of our place, (slaves), called upon the Intendent of our town, Mr. John B. Cleveland, and presented him with a fine glass Pitcher and Bowl as a token of their respect for him personally, and their high appreciation of his administration as Intendent. . . . Such tokens we regard as emblematic of the fidelity of our slaves and a decided reprobation of the infamous proclamation of Abraham Lincoln." The *Spartan* was trying to bolster the confidence of its readers that President Lincoln's Emancipation Proclamation would have no effect on the purported reliability of Spartanburg District's slave population. By 1864 the newspaper was beginning to publish news of upcoming executions of slaves sentenced by the Magistrates' and Freeholders' Court, something it had not bothered to do before.[28] In addition, whereas the newspaper often had published advertisements offering "Negroes to Hire" early during the war, in 1864 it ran many more advertisements for the sale of real property and of slaves. Until the war the sale of slaves had rarely been advertised in the village's newspaper, but during the war such advertisements steadily grew in number and in the size of the print used. Late in 1864 and even in the early months of 1865 advertisements for the sale of "Negroes" became plentiful and apparently they were successful as few appeared more than once. Indeed, Meta Grimball, a refugee in the village, commented in her diary that the trade in slaves was brisk.[29]

During antebellum times some white people drove some slaves to ignore the consequences of offering resistance. During the war it appears that such situations continued, and in the atmosphere of heightened anxiety such reactions among slaves may have become even more common. In 1864 one overseer, who was having trouble controlling a slave woman whom he wanted to whip, hit her twice with a stick and succeeded in tying her up. She yelled to a young boy to run fetch her husband who, when he arrived from the field, swore he would "die or Commit murder" if she was not released. The husband and another slave swore "that she was their Colour, and when ever at any time, they found one of their Colour tied they would unloose or set them free at the risk of their life's." Yelling "hang shoot and bedamned" they set upon the overseer and cut the woman free. In this case the slave men were punished with three hundred lashes with a piece of cow hide, the lashes to be administered seventy-five at a time once a week until completed. The woman received seventy-five lashes.[30]

Slaves sometimes were in altercations with each other.[31] In 1864 a slave named Ted reported that while he was making a line of fence with another slave named Sam, Ted became aware of Sam's bad temper. In order to avoid conflict Ted moved to another place. Sam came up and tore down what Ted had built saying it was badly done. After some angry words Sam hit Ted twice with a rail, and when Ted saw Sam rushing him again he hit Sam with a piece of railing he had in his hand. Unfortunately the rail had a nail running through it which struck Sam on the head and killed him. Ted ran to his master for assistance but lied about the events for fear of his master's temper. Ted told the court that "his master will sometimes when excited fly into a passion and act with a great deal of violence, draws his gun and threatens to shoot his negroes and he [Ted] thought this was one of the times he would be certain to shoot." The owner's son corroborated Ted's story and explained to the court that "when his Father is drinking he is excitable and violent among his negroes and frequently threatens to shoot them. Such was his condition last week [at the time of the incident], at such times . . . [the slaves] are in great dread of him." The court found Ted not guilty of murder but sentenced him to one hundred lashes for killing Sam.[32]

During the war the tendency to impose harsher sentences in the Magistrates Court was evident. Even during the 1850s a trend emerged to dismiss fewer cases for lack of evidence. An increasing number of the accusations resulted in adjudication. In addition, the percentage of guilty verdicts rose. In the little over four years of the war the total number of guilty verdicts was only seven shy of the total for the entire decade of the 1850s, and the number of cases resulting in severe punishments (over one hundred lashes) was six higher. Extreme punishments meted out by the courts grew larger in each succeeding decade: the average number of lashes in the 1840s was 178 lashes, in the 1850s it was 227, and in the 1860s it was 337. During the antebellum period and even more so during the war, many citizens became increasingly anxious about and fearful of the slave population. As control over the circumstances of their own daily lives broke down because of the multiple pressures of wartime, masters began to see conspiracies behind every infraction of the rules. As fears grew so did the number of court cases. Magistrates seemed reluctant to dismiss accusations and preferred to let the freeholders on the jury sort them out, and the severity of the sentences grew.

The growing apprehension among many slave owners about the war's impact on the institution of slavery is evident in the increasingly harsh sentences passed on during the war by the Freeholder's Court for what would have been considered relatively mild infractions during the antebellum period. A few examples will serve to illustrate the growing anxiety:

Case No. 239, Oct 14, 1861 Assault and Battery and Insolent language. Sentence—"20 strips today on pure back with cowhide or switch. 3 months imprisonment in Dist. Jail and Recd 25 strips each salesday making 75 strips or the 3 months imprisonment + 75 strips be remitted provided the prisoner Sy [Josiah] will return immediately to the Mess that had him in employ heretofore at Camp Johnson + remain with and in their service dureing their enlistment or term of service."

Case No. 240, February 20, 1862 Selling spirituous liquors—sentence: "39 lashes each sales day" [second Monday of every month] "from Feb. to July then jail until January 1863"

Case No. 242, April 10, 1862 "Thornton, you stand indicted for having on the night of the 6th of March last broken open the store house of C A. Waters, and feloniously taken stolen and carried away therefrom several pairs of boots & shoes, 1 pair cassimere pants, 3 shirts, 2 vests, several pocket books and purses, a Gingham dress, 2 neck socks, 1 pair gloves, 1 quilt & 1 blanket. . . ." The court decided that he receive "four hundred lashes, 200 today & that he be in Spartanburg jail until the 19th inst. And then receive 200 lashes on the bare back & be delivered to his owner given under our hands."

Case No. 243, 16 April 1862 75 lashes for stealing hog meat from Mr. Zimmerman [a prominent hotel owner and industrialist].

Case No. 244, 21 April 1862 "For stealing, taking, and carrying away one Baking Pan, and one Petty Coat." Sentence of 50 lashes.

Case No. 255 Christene was found not guilty of burning a stable; "in most of the witnesses agst her they speak of her 'saucy talk;'" she is found not guilty of burning stables but in Case 256, 31 June 1863 this same Christene is found guilty of "a misdeameanor on Monday the 22nd of June 1863 by offering threats and speaking disrespectfully of and in regard to his [Edgar Falk] wife Isabella Falk without just cause. . . ." found guilty even though ["That the insolence was provoked by questions propounded"] and sentenced "at the common jail of the District the bare back—Twenty-eight lashes well laid on."

Case 272, 16 March 1864 Isaac Waddell a free person of color "for being concerned in distilling contrary to law" guilty "that he is to be imprisoned until next Monday morning and to receive Fifty lashes on his first entering the jail this the 16th day of March with a strap will laid on his bare back and Fifty more on Monday morning next."

Case 275, 19 April 1864 Laura Wilson testified that "near William Layton's spring in said district assault and catch hold of her shoulder with his hand, she jerked loose from him, he said Henry, did then stop before her and picked up a rock and drew his knife and told her if she moved or hallowed he would kill her and she told him she would hallow if he did not let her alone she then started on her way and said Henry ran off and told her if she would not say any about the matter he would let her alone she went on and he disturbed her no farther." Accused pleaded guilty at trial. "sentence him to receive 700 lashes well laid on, two hundred fifty today 200 lashes this day two weeks, and 250 lashes on this day four weeks to be inflicted on the bare skin of the priosoner with a whip, rope, strap or any suitable instrument to two last instalments to be inflicted at Martin Hopkins shop."

Case 295, deposition 22 Feb 1865 "did on Sunday night the 19th inst. Go the house of Mrs Daniel Johnson & grossly & wantonly insult & disturb her by ordering their suppers & their horse to be fed." Testimony of Mrs. Johnson: "& swore they come there to be accommodated in Every Way & that they were Drunk & Swore in Such a Manner as alarmed her so that she left her home to their mercy. Came their about 9 oclock at night on the 19th Feb '65 Remained about 1 hour" Three accused received 50, 39 and 20 lashes respectively.[33]

As some citizens became desperate at the growing prospect of defeat they took out their frustrations on the perpetrators of the most immediate threats to their order. A striking example occurred in 1864 when a court, for the crime of stealing bacon, one hat, a looking glass, a bottle of soda, and a cake of tallow, sentenced two slaves "to be hung by the Neck until they are *Dead*," a sentence reserved before the war for murder or arson.[34]

In October 1865 (six months after the war ended) in the last case before the Magistrates and Freeholders Court there was a foreboding testimony by a free African American woman. She spoke about her husband Bob who had also always been a free African American: "Four white men came to Bob's house and told [him] . . . that he [was] . . . in a scrape and wanted [him] . . . to go with them . . . & clear himself and [he] . . . went off with them. A short time after they left she heard some one hollor. The moon was one hour high when they left. She started to Layton's early this morning, but seeing the horse tracks where they had turned out of the road she followed and found [Bob] . . . hanging dead to a limb of a small chestnut oak tree."[35]

This vigilante killing of a free African American was a sad foreshadowing of similar events during the next one hundred years of segregation. The Civil War brought freedom to the enslaved, but it did not bring civil rights or the protection of laws. All of that would have to wait for over one hundred more years.

INDIVIDUALS

PART TWO

The following stories are about individual residents of Spartanburg District during the Civil War. The tales provide insight into the impact of war on even the smallest of communities, whether the sites of battles or not. People make history and historians largely deal with people in the aggregate, for the national and regional narrative is the sum of the actions and reactions of individuals. Here the focus is on some of the more compelling individual components of Spartanburg's overall story, which humanize and enhance its larger narrative.

These narratives, whether their endings are known or unknown, happened and deserve to be told: the plight of a slave suffering the terrors of the institution into which she was born, the struggle of a war widow managing her husband's farm operation under arduous circumstances, the animosity and unforeseen violence of public accusations of treason, and the trauma of having to leave a comfortable way of life for relative poverty and an alien social world. All were part of the complexity of wartime Spartanburg District.

War is devastating for those on the battlefield and those at home. For the residents of Spartanburg during the Civil War the impact missed almost no one, no matter how far removed they were from battle or how loyal they were to the new nation. Their stories reflect the delicate bedrock of the Confederacy.

5

The Slave Catherine and the Kindness of Strangers?

On the 25th of January, 1865, David Lipscomb, a resident of Northern Spartanburg District, formally accused his slave, Catherine, before the local magistrate, Davis Moore, of the crime of arson.[1] The magistrate summoned eight local slave holders to appear at David Lipscomb's farm on the first day of February 1865 for Catherine's trial. On that day in February five of the eight freeholders were chosen to act as judge and jury to try Catherine on the indictment which accused her of "maliciously burning his [David Lipscomb's] stables, four head of horses & a quantity of fodder & shucks."[2]

According to the trial records Catherine pled guilty; her trial proceeded immediately with the hearing of witnesses "she had to produce in her behalf as well as those against her." The court record indicates no witnesses on Catherine's behalf and the following account by the witnesses against her:

> Evidence in behalf of the State. J. C. Humphries sworn says that he was at Mr. Lipscomb on Saturday after the burning & being requested by Mr Lipscomb to go upstairs wher Catherine was that he accordingly done so in company with Mr. S. Littlejohn for the purpose of examing the girl. That she upon being interrogated by them she acknowledged that she took fire from her Mother's house and sot fire to the chalf near the stables. That there was no other person present with her at the time she sot fire to the chalf. That she further said that her sister Silah went with her a part of [the] way with her when she started with the fire & went with her as far as the kiln[,] her sister discovering the fire asked her where she was going & she told her she was going to the stable that her sister stopped & would not go any further, that her mother knew when she went out of the house with the fire & said to her ["]you are going to do some

devilment,["] that some time previous to that she heard her Mother say that her master had a full smoke house but she would not be surprised if [he] was to get up some morning & find it in coals, that her Uncle Mose sanctioned what her Mother had said.

Samuel Littlejohn sworn says that he was present with Mr. Humphries at the time when the prisoner was examined by them, that he fully concurs with Mr. Humphries in the statement he has made as being fully correct.[3]

The "Court after mature consideration found the prisoner Guilty" and sentenced her to be hanged between the hours of twelve and two o'clock on Friday the 24th of February, 1865.[4] Thus far the case seems ordinary as the accused pled guilty, and the state mandated death by hanging as the punishment for arson by a slave. However, things were not quite so straight forward as the court record indicated.

In February 1865, Andrew Magrath, governor of South Carolina, was in Spartanburg where he had fled from the state capitol, Columbia, when he realized that General William T. Sherman and his Union army were headed in that direction. Among Governor McGrath's papers in the South Carolina State Archives is a petition from people in Spartanburg District asking him to pardon Catherine. The petition is dated March 28, 1865. The records of Catherine's trial which normally should be found amongst the records of the Spartanburg Magistrates and Freeholders Court are found among the governor's papers.[5] The petition is signed by seventy-four residents of Spartanburg District, including at least two of David Lipscomb's immediate neighbors. Among the signers of the petition are Davis Moore (the owner of nineteen slaves), the magistrate with whom David Lipscomb filed his complaint and who acted as prosecutor in the case, and that of J. H. Garrison who was one of the jurors at the trial. The trial records are among Governor Magrath's papers probably because the magistrate, Davis Moore, sent them to the governor along with the petition.

This remarkable document requesting a pardon for Catherine bears investigation, for it contains information which does not appear in the trial records. The magistrate may have sent the court papers along with the petition in order to highlight these omissions.

We might begin a study of this case by asking who Catherine was. The petition emphasizes her youth. Among David Lipscomb's twenty-three slaves listed in the 1860 Slave Census were twelve females, six adults ranging in age from twenty-one to sixty, and six youngsters ranging in age from four to thirteen. On the census record there is a mark in the box for "idiots" beside the notation for the twenty-seven year old. The mark looks like a black dot and may be an imperfection or an accidental drop of ink. The mark is unlike the other marks made by the census taker. It is most likely that one of the three female slaves whose ages were given as thirteen, twelve, and ten in 1860 was the unfortunate Catherine, as they would have been eighteen, seventeen, and fifteen in 1865. Since the census does not list the names of the slaves there is no way to be sure of Catherine's age, but given her planning and the conversation she supposedly had with her sister, Silah, Catherine probably was seventeen or eighteen.

The trial record tells us nothing about Catherine or any mitigating circumstances having to do with her alleged crime. Since she freely confessed her guilt, we might wonder what motivated her to commit arson, one of only two crimes which, when perpetrated by slaves, carried the death penalty. We get some inkling as to her situation and motivation through a comment made in the petition: when a "minister of the gospel who visits her, asked her if she would like to be pardoned and return to her master, she replied that death would be preferable to such treatment as she had been subjected to."[6]

Furthermore, the petitioners describe Catherine not only as young but also of a "weak condition of mind." Catherine claims that "her illtreatment by her master was of so aggravated a nature, as almost to deprive her of the little rationality she naturally possesses." Indeed, the petition makes a point of claiming that her youth and "weak condition of mind" make it "evident that she was not conscious of committing a felony." Also the petitioners point out that Catherine set fire to a straw house and that the fire then spread to the stable, insinuating that she had no intention of firing the stables themselves. The petitioners also assert that Catherine claims her "purpose was only to divert the attention of her master, who had been whipping her severely, and her object was to create an excitement, which would give her a short respite"—a claim they believe. Only in the petition do we learn what she so badly wanted a respite from: maintaining that Lipscomb's "reputation for cruelty to his slaves is well known," the petitioners claim that Catherine's body "bears the marks of laceration and the scars on her limbs shew cruel treatment," which gives credence to the desperation evident in Catherine's statement to the minister.

This is all the information we have about this incident, and it is unsatisfactory. At the very least, we want to know whether Governor Magrath pardoned Catherine. Did she live or did she die? History does not always provide answers. On the disposition of Catherine's case the records are silent. We know the petition and the trial record are amongst the governor's papers, but we do not know if he read them, or how he may have acted upon the request.

Nevertheless there is much to learn from these events. Like all slaves, young Catherine lived at the mercy of her master and so the conditions of her life depended on the disposition and character of her owner. Unfortunately for Catherine, her master was characterized as a mean-spirited and cruel person. We know that David Lipscomb lived in the Limestone Springs area of the Northern part of Spartanburg, was age fifty-six in 1864, was married to a forty-three year old woman named Mary, that they had seven children, and that he owned a plantation and twenty-three slaves.[7] Some of his neighbors charged that Catherine, being of a "weak condition of mind" to begin with, was so ill-treated by her master as to almost deprive her of what little sanity she had, although she had sense enough to devise a plan to provide herself a respite.

We should also note that the evidence of her master's treatment includes the phrase "the scars on her limbs." Actually that is an unusual phrase, as one would expect scars on her back (female slaves were not spared the lash because of gender) but not on her arms and legs. Normally, whippings were preceded by tying the victim to a tree or other object by wrapping their arms around it, or suspending them by their arms. In any case the immobilization of the arms was necessary so the body would be exposed for punishment, it being the largest target. Yet the petitioners make a special point of mentioning the "scars on her limbs," so they must have been numerous—over seventy people signed the document and would have had to agree to the emphasis.

Catherine's scars could have resulted from countless means. Numerous scars on her arms and legs may have come from whippings administered by an intoxicated man whose control was not good. The end of the lash may have bitten into her limbs as it curled haphazardly about her body. Or the scars could have resulted from random blows inflicted with objects that were close at hand. Lipscomb's son testified that his father often threatened his slaves with a revolver. Such blows might cause the victim to raise her arms for protection. The presence of such scars invokes the image of a young, feeble-minded girl, attempting to crawl away after having been knocked to the ground as her attacker rains blows down upon her.

What we can surmise is that Catherine, beaten unmercifully, and possibly feeble-minded, wanted finally to end her ordeal. The petition does not contest the guilty verdict; rather it seeks mercy through a pardon based on Lipscomb's treatment and Catherine's condition.

Many people believed arson to be a favored weapon of retribution for slaves because it did great harm without necessarily killing anyone, and any evidence which might identify the perpetrator was likely to be consumed in the flames. Was Catherine bright enough to think of this possibility? Was she capable of such meticulous planning? The petitioners' comment about how she was nearly deprived of her sanity indicates that they believed she was, at least, responsible for the fire. They also seemed to believe that no fully sane person would perpetrate such a crime and willingly admit her guilt, so Catherine must have been out of her right mind when she acted as she did. This was easy to believe, they implied, when you consider how David Lipscomb treated her.

Finally, the petition makes Catherine's wish to never return to her owner absolutely clear. She preferred death to such a result. Catherine revealed her wishes on this matter to a white minister who "visits her."[8] Although Catherine is said to be "of a weak condition of mind," the petition gives the firm impression that she clearly understood what returning to David Lipscomb meant. Nevertheless the petition only asks for a pardon. Given Catherine's emphatic statement that she prefers death to being returned to her master, the petition does not ask for anything that would have removed her from Lipscomb's control, such as her sale. Although the petition appears magnanimous, it also seems unsatisfactory. If successful it would likely have resulted in just what Catherine feared the most. Given the care with which the petition was crafted and the trouble its sponsors underwent in collecting so many signatures, it is strange that they did not ask for some form of protection for Catherine from her master.

The court had set the date for Catherine's execution for the 24th of February, but the petition is dated the 28th of March so the execution obviously had not taken place. Since the magistrate who presided over the trial was sponsoring the petition, perhaps the date of execution was delayed in order to have time to gather signatures. Also, the end of the Civil War was imminent, it would end in April of 1865, and the petitioners may have considered the long term results of a pardon moot. In any case, let us now examine the people who provided us with the mitigating circumstances of this case: the petitioners.

Of the seventy-four persons who signed the petition, no information could be found on eighteen.[9] Of the fifty-six people who could be identified, thirty were slaveholders. The number of slaves owned ranged from one to twenty-six with thirteen of the slaveholders owning more than ten slaves. Only eight of David Lipscomb's neighbors signed the petition, which may appear to be a small number, but there were eighteen Lipscomb slaveholding family farms in the immediate vicinity of David's land. Their dominance of the area may have discouraged some neighbors from signing the petition. However, David's nearest neighbor, Lemuel Farnandez, who owned twenty-six slaves, and another close neighbor, J. H. Garrison, who owned one slave and who had been a juror at Catherine's trial, did sign the petition.

The twenty-nine residents of Spartanburg village who signed the petition were a varied group. The petition sponsors would have wanted to make an impression on the governor, and they succeeded in having several prominent persons sign on—three physicians, a former congressman, the president of a local bank, one of the editors of the local newspaper, a state representative, eighteen Confederate veterans, and fifteen businessmen. Some of these businessmen were involved in local politics and would have been known to Governor Magrath. Magrath had visited Spartanburg on several occasions and had participated in large meetings with the citizens of the village to help stir up enthusiasm for separation from the Union. The businessmen ranged from craftsmen and owners of small stores to influential entrepreneurs. There were also several persons involved in education including Warren DuPré, a professor at Wofford College, who owned sixteen slaves.

In addition, nineteen residents of the southern part of the district signed the petition. These people came from all over that part of Spartanburg. They may have known of David Lipscomb—they likely knew of the Lipscomb clan—or were persuaded by the content of the petition. Given the variety of persons who signed the document and how scattered they were over the area, it is likely that Davis Moore left it in the court house for some time so anyone who happened to come by could read and sign it if they so desired.

An 1880s photograph of "Morgan Square" showing the dominance, even at that late era, of the 1856 court house. The spring that was crucial to the decision to select this place as the center of the District was located just behind the Court House. The buildings on the right side of the photograph were built after the Civil War. Photograph courtesy of the Herald-Journal Willis Collection, Spartanburg County Public Libraries, South Carolina.

However, none of Spartanburg District's most influential politicians nor any owners of the largest plantations or most slaves (for example, Simpson Bobo, H. H. Thompson, John Winsmith, E. P. Smith, John C. Zimmerman) signed the petition. These men were politically active and lived in or came to the village frequently and certainly would have had the opportunity to sign.

The people who did sign asserted that Lipscomb's "reputation for cruelty to his slaves is well known." This is a startling admission, for it means that at least some of the petitioners knew of the conditions on David Lipscomb's farm. In spite of Lipscomb's cruelty, and the evidence that the petition itself puts forth for the governor's consideration, Spartanburg's residents had done nothing about Lipscomb's behavior. There were laws in South Carolina, as in other Southern states, meant to protect slaves from such abuse. But in the case of slaves, the protection of private property appears to have been more important than the protection of human life and limb. Before the neighbors were willing to take action against Lipscomb, the extremes of his farm had to place Catherine's life in the balance.

These petitioners may have saved this one girl, but the true meaning of the episode lies in the degree of cruelty it took before neighbors acted. This petition is aimed at saving one slave; there is no evidence that anyone intervened on behalf of the rest of Lipscomb's human property. This could indicate that by 1865 people knew that the war was ending and that slavery would soon be abolished by the terms of the Emancipation Proclamation of 1863, so there was no need to do more. The belief that a person has the absolute right to do with his property what he pleases was strong in the South, but its implications for the slaves were frightening.

As a slave Catherine had rights, although she may not even have been aware of it. Yet, having legal rights did not ensure that she could benefit from or exercise those rights. These rights had been articulated in the 1740 codification of laws governing slaves and their owners, and refined in several acts of the South Carolina legislature passed between 1740 and 1860. In 1848, in a speech given at the State Agricultural Society Semi-Annual Meeting in Spartanburg, South Carolina appeals court judge John Belton O'Neall had reviewed and criticized all the South Carolina laws having to do with slaves.[10] O'Neall was a highly respected judge. The Society published his speech as a pamphlet, and directed that it "be submitted to the Governor with a request that he would lay it before the Legislature, at its approaching Session, November, 1848" so that body could consider the judge's suggestions for possible changes in the state's slave laws. The legislature took no such action. Nevertheless O'Neall's contemporary commentary is the most comprehensive and critical document written on South Carolina slave laws.

The Commons House of Assembly passed "An Act for the Better Ordering and Governing Negroes and other Slaves in this Province" in 1740. This act remained fundamental to the "Ordering and Governing [of] Negroes and other Slaves" in South Carolina throughout the antebellum years. The preamble to the act of 1740 defined "slaves" as "property in the hands of particular persons, the extent of whose power over such slaves ought to be settled and limited by positive laws . . . [such that] the owners and other persons having the care and government of slaves may be restrained from exercising too great rigour and cruelty over them."[11] The act went on to describe in detail how slaves ought to be controlled and for what and how they should be punished. It is important to note that the assembly also had in mind both the advantages and the responsibilities that came with slaveholding as they addressed the protection of slaves several times throughout the Act. For instance, the assembly maintained "That if any negro or other slave, who shall be employed in the lawful business or service of his master, owner, overseer, or other person having charge of such slave, shall be beaten, bruised, maimed or disabled by any person or persons not having sufficient cause or lawful authority for so doing, (of which cause the justices of the peace, respectively, may judge)"[12] the offending person or persons would be punished. Further on, the assembly made even clearer its intent by holding "That if any slave shall suffer in life, limb or member, or shall be maimed, beaten or abused, contrary to the directions and true intent and meaning of this Act . . . the owner or other person who shall have the care and government of such slave, and in whose possession or power such slave shall be, shall be deemed . . . to be guilty of such offence, and shall be proceeded against accordingly."[13] Those who wrote the law went to great lengths to make certain that just provocations by slaves justified harsh penalties. They also showed that there were punishments inflicted and behaviors exhibited by masters that crossed the line—it was just punishment they sought, not cruelty.

In his 1848 commentary on slave law, John Belton O'Neall dealt with the rights of slaves in various places. He stated: "Although slaves, by Act of 1740, are declared to be chattels personal, yet, they are also in our law, considered as persons with many rights, and liabilities, civil and criminal."[14] And of course, the idea that slaves were a particular kind of property was the crux of the matter. They were human beings and needed to be treated as such according to the dictates of civilization. O'Neall, in mentioning beatings, went on to say: "So if the beating be either without provocation, or is so enormous that the provocation can be no excuse, then it is unlawful."[15]

O'Neall maintained that slave owners or others guilty of scandalous offenses against slaves—including if a slave was "cruelly beaten or abused"—did not suffer severe enough punishment under the laws in existence in 1848. The judge explained that under an 1821 law a person who inflicted such punishment could exculpate themselves by oath, which in his view permitted "the greatest temptation every presented to perjury,"[16] and recommended that the law be amended. In further discussing the well-being of slaves, O'Neall wrote: "For as the master is bound by the most solemn obligation to protect his slaves from suffering, he is bound by the same obligation to defray the expenses or services of another to preserve the life of his slave, or to relieve the slave from pain and danger. *The slave lives for his master's service. His time, his labor, his comforts, are all at his master's disposal.* The duty of humane treatment and of medical assistance, (when clearly necessary) ought not to be withholden."[17] In one of his most ironic comments O'Neall, in mentioning the effect of strengthening protections for slaves, maintained: "They [the slaves] know *now* that the shield of the law is over them, and thus protected, they yield a more hearty obedience and effective service to their masters."[18] Although perhaps true for some slaves, such a view was certainly not shared by Catherine.

By ordering the publication of Judge O'Neall's commentary for the legislature's use, Spartanburg's members of the Agricultural Society publicly endorsed the judge's views as early as 1848. That resolution seems, in light of Catherine's case, to have had no more practical effect on district residents than it did on the legislature. Many of the laws meant to protect slaves were merely emotional and intellectual exercises.

David Lipscomb was a man who, even in an age when American society condoned the practice, should not have owned human property. Catherine was a person who should not have been owned by anyone, much less David Lipscomb. But slaves did not choose their masters. Lipscomb's neighbors and their supporters went on record taking a position against a fellow slaveholder and on behalf of a slave. That action, rare as it was, preserved an incident that spoke volumes about the ultimate failure of efforts to protect the "humanity"—Judge O'Neall's word—of the institution of slavery.

Petition[,] Spartanburg 28th March 1865
    To His Excellency Gov. A. G. Magrath
    The petition of the undersigned citizens and residents of Spartanburg sheweth—That "Caroline" slave of "David Lipscomb" under sentence of death for setting fire to an outbuilding on the premises of her master, in their opinion is an object for the exercise of Executive clemency, for reasons which we beg leave to submit to your consideration. From her youth and weak condition

of mind, it is evident that she was not conscious of committing a felony, and she states that her illtreatment by her master was of so aggravated a nature, as almost to deprive her of the little rationality she naturally posesses. This statement of illtreatment is evidenced by the condition of her body which bears the marks of laceration, and the scars on her limbs shews cruel treatment. The neighbors of her master also testify, that his reputation for cruelty to his slaves is well known. The house set on fire by her, was a straw house, which communicated the fire to the stable. She says her purpose, was only to divert the attention of her master, who had been whipping her severely, and her object was to create an excitement, which would give her a short respite.

The minister of the gospel who visits her, asked her, if she would like to be pardoned and return to her master, she replied—that death would be preferable to such treatment as she had been subjected to.

As no one lived in the house burned the question has arisen, whether the crime is one that comes under the head of felony.

Considering her youth & sex—her ignorance & feeble state of mind, also the provocation given her, and the nature of the offence, your petitioners humbly pray that she be pardoned by your excellency.

(signed)

J. W. Garrett Lld	Joseph Foster	J. J. Boyd	A. P. Smith
T. Stobo Farrow	B. H. Neighbours	J. W. White	
Hiram Mitchell	F. B. Anderson	Wm. K. Blake	Chas Thompson
Henry Abbotts	H. E. Heinisch	Fred Fanning	Marcus Kirby
Chain Allen	I. Hastes	C. Thompson	A. W. Bivings
William Choice	R. H. Foster	A. W. Walker	J. A. Lee
Warren DuPré	David W. Moore	W. H. Fleming	
J. H. Goss	J. B. Cleveland	W. Shiver	F. Tepfre
L. Pintts	A. H. Kirby	R. W. Folger	P. T. Smith
Nathan A. Holmes	Lee L. Smith	Thomas O. P. Vernon	
James Phillips	Briant Cash	John Turnur	J. W. Webber
Lemuel A. Farnandez	B. G. Lambright	Joseph Richards	
J. S. Land	B. O. Turner	Jones W. Foster	Wm Westbrook
T. T. Wilkins	M. M. Gossett	J. S. Rountree	R. Lanford
J. G. Carter	John Keast	J. A. Fowler	D. C. Judd
J. W. Hanckel	Wm Irwin	O. P. McArthur	A. Smythe

W. D. Wilkins	W. D. Beverly	M. K. Johnstone	I. S. Hanckel
Davis Moore Mag.	J. H. Garrison Juror	James Hanckel	
J. E. Godgion	P. G. Kirby	B. F. Lambright	D. G. Finley
J. C. Wall	A. Bumpus	G. W. Watkins	

Emily Lyles Harris,
Reluctant Farmer

Emily Lyles Harris's husband, David Harris, started a journal in 1855 to keep an accurate record of his farm work so he could eventually learn the very best time and method for undertaking his various tasks. With his wife, children, and ten slaves, he worked one hundred acres of a five hundred acre farm located eight miles southeast of the village of Spartanburg. In addition to recording his daily work, David often used his journal to comment on current affairs, family life, and his own state of mind. His records tell us much about farm life in the county, for he was a diligent and perceptive witness.

Any investigation into the state of mind of people in Spartanburg District during the Civil War must also pay particular attention to Emily Harris. When David eventually went off to war, he asked his wife to carry on with his journal. He did us a great favor, for Emily made the journal her confidante. To it she confided her feelings, her opinions, and her fears. Through the entries in her journal we catch a glimpse of what it was like to be the wife of a farmer and of a soldier during much of the Civil War. There is no better contemporary record of life in Spartanburg District and few comparable records for the region. Emily was an introspective and brutally honest commentator who looked at herself and her world unsparingly.

Born in 1827, Emily Jane Lyles Harris grew up in Spartanburg village. In 1840 her parents moved to the country. Her father, Amos Lyles, was intent on educating his only daughter, and Emily soon found herself boarding in the village so she might attend Phoebe Paine's school. Phoebe Paine was a Yankee schoolteacher who believed that women should be educated to use their intellectual gifts. In later years Emily recalled Phoebe Paine admonishing her to remember her "buried talent."[1] Historians of Spartanburg owe Phoebe Paine much, if for

Emily Lyles Harris. Courtesy of
Wofford College Library Archives.

no other reason than preparing Emily Lyles to write well, with feeling and understanding about herself and her times.

Emily Harris had nine children. When war broke out a set of twins had already died and her six remaining children were ages four, six, eight, ten, twelve,
and fourteen. She was thirty-three years old. In 1862 she gave birth to her seventh
and last child. Since her marriage in 1846, Emily's life had been filled with giving
birth to and raising her children, sometimes teaching them, making their clothes,
and tending a garden which provided much of the food for the family. She had at
least one house servant to help her. Although she enjoyed church, attended some
social functions, and frequently received relatives at home, she did not often go
to the village or other destinations. Her elderly mother lived with her for a few
years in the late 1850s. With all these responsibilities she mainly stayed at home,
and there is evidence that she was not altogether content. Her husband, David,
often complained of her temper, which irritated him; they seem to have quarreled
often. Emily's temper affected everyone on the farm, for she was sometimes angry
enough to whip her female slaves and she whipped a male slave at least once.

Such frequent outbursts may partly have been a response to the isolation of the
farm, which did not provide the family much diversion to relieve the monotony
of their rural existence. It was ironic that this isolation, of which both Harrises
complained, also did not afford them any personal privacy. In 1862 David Harris
wrote:

Solitude sometimes is my most pleasant companion. How nice it is to sit in a quiet room by a glowing fire of shining embers, and to live over the past and to mark out pleasant plans for the future. This is a pleasure almost entirely denied me. So many children, and many cares. Oftentimes I would sit by the fire, and read and wright and dream. But children will be children, and children will make a noise. Then my resort is the bed. To find rest for my wearied limbs, and my diseased boddy. Wife often asks me to remain up with her, but I am compelled to take refuge in the bed, until I have become so accustomed to retiring early, that I cannot well do otherwise.

David wrote this entry at a time when Emily was also feeling overburdened and depressed, but he made no mention of her need for the same privacy and solitude that he craved. Nor did he seem to understand her need for his adult company. He was shutting her out, isolating her even more, and finding his peace, such as it was, partly at her expense. In the war's later years Emily confided to the journal that she "craved a few quiet days and for several weeks they have been denied me. I may as well give it up and resign myself to live in hub-bub all my life." A few days later Emily voiced a general human complaint when she lamented that her seven "children have all been at home. I have been much troubled by their noise and confusion which has caused me to ask myself what I should do with them when the school was out, and then what I should do with myself if I had no children." Farm life was a paradox. These two adults did not seem to be able to find sufficient companionship in each other, and the press of humanity which resulted from nine people living in a small house (two small rooms with a sleeping attic and a very small attached kitchen) only added to their frustration and anxiety. The farm was isolated, but the people were never alone.[2]

When David Harris learned that his departure for service with the state volunteers was imminent he worried about leaving his family. He was sure Emily would care for the children and that she would work conscientiously and hard, but he also knew she would "be much at a loss with the management of the farm and the negroes." She had never had to assume the responsibility for the operation of everything and now, all of a sudden, it was dropped in her lap. He knew she would try, and he was ready to accept the consequences, whatever they might be. Emily was not quite so reconciled:

The trial has come at last, my husband has gone to the war, he left me yesterday afternoon. I thought I would rather not go with him to the depot but after he had gone I felt an almost irresistible impulse to follow him and keep his beloved countenance in my sight as long as possible. It was a hard parting, a bitter farewell. Ninety days, how long to be without him, how long for him to bear the privations and hardships of the camp and . . . how I shudder to think I may never see him again. A load of responsibilities are resting upon me in his absence but I shall be found trying to bear them as well as I can.[3]

Among her difficulties was one faced by all mothers whose husbands are away for long periods of time—how to deal with the children. These were farm children used to having both their parents with them, or nearby, almost all the time. The younger children did not understand David Harris's long absence. One child, his father's namesake, in anger about something ran from the house to the gate "expecting to be taken up by his father. The tears would come a little in spite of one but I choked them down because the children seem sad enough." Emily controlled her emotions to help her children adjust, but the sensitivity, good nature, and deep feelings she showed in doing so rewarded her unkindly. Troubled and unsettled though she was, others among her relatives and friends turned to her for support. To them she was a strong woman, a realistic woman, a woman who could cope. Such had always been her role, and she was sought out, ironically, for the very comfort and advice, the intimate sharing she herself so desperately needed. During a visit by a relative grieving a husband off to war, Emily had to "laugh and be gay on her account." She was the one to whom many turned, and thus "it has always been my lot to be obliged to shut up my griefs in my own breast." As it turned out she could manage the farm better than she could manage her griefs.[4]

Even when Emily felt she had things under control her journal entries are marked with sadness and a depressing sense of foreboding and loss: "All going well as far as I can judge but tonight it is raining and cold and a soldier's wife cannot be happy in bad weather or during a battle. All the afternoon as it clouded up I felt gloomy and sad and could not help watching the gate for a gray horse and its rider but he came not, though all his family are sheltered and comfortable the one who prepared the comfort is lying far away with scanty covering and poor shelter." Most of the time she did not feel under control but overwhelmed. Her days were full ones; she felt almost crushed by the myriad things she had to do: "It has rained all day, the children have been cross and ungovernable. Old Judah and Edom [slaves] were both sick. Ann [slave] is trying to weave, and a poor weave it is, the sewing must be done, everything must be attended to, Laura is coughing a rough ominous cough, has scarcely any shoes on her feet, and no hope of getting any this week. West has the croup. I am trying to wean the baby and the cows laid out last night, and last and worst of all I know my husband is somewhere miserably cold, wet, and comfortless."[5] No matter how badly things went for her, Emily always thought of David, and she took some comfort in the fact that he wrote her every day.[6]

Emily did settle into the routine of running the farm, and some of her journal entries sound much like those of her husband. She planted, complained of the weather, meticulously recorded all the data of farm life her husband so cherished, constantly berated her slaves and, unlike her husband, always recorded the health of the children. "Family not well, negroes doing nothing but eating, making fires and wearing out clothes," was a typical entry. But she did grow crops, and grow them well. She had to hire extra field hands to help her bring in the harvest, although hiring was difficult; no one wanted money, everyone wanted food. Her record crop of oats—the best in her area of the district—almost went to ruin in the field because she had to pay her hired hands in wheat and she almost ran out. She exhausted everyone including herself in getting the oats in.

Yet, even her successes took their toll. Her persistence was in spite of herself. "I shall never get used to being left as the head of affairs at home. The burden is very heavy, and there is no one to smile on me as I trudge wearily along in the dark with it. I am constituted so as to crave a guide and protector. I am not an independent woman nor ever shall be." Emily felt insecure and incompetent, but to everyone around her she appeared just the opposite. She did get everything done but despaired of the life it meant she had to lead and the strength she had to conjure up: "I am busy cutting our winter clothing, every thing is behind time and I'm tired to death with urging children and negroes to work."[7]

The pressures of farm, slaves, and family were almost too much. By late 1863 Emily was beginning to hate the farm, despair of her life, and fear herself: "If I am always to live as I have lived the last few months I shall soon tire of life and be willing to die. It seems that I have to think for every one on the place. . . . Every little thing has to pass through my hands in some way." Assailed as she was by self-doubt, a lack of privacy, and the burdens of responsibility, it is not surprising that the war itself began to take on an evil aspect for her. She blamed her husband's absence on the government, a government which she came to resent. In the spring of 1864 David Harris tried to get out of the army by securing an exemption as a farmer, but he was turned down. "Now of course there is no hope but for him to remain and fight our foes," she wrote, but she felt as much "like fighting our men who, standing at the head of affairs, are the cause of keeping such as him in the field, as I do the Yankees." This is self-pity; there were thousands like him and thousands like her. Her skepticism about the war grew until in 1865 she was openly hoping for a quick defeat. When she heard of a battle that was won by the Confederates she commented that it "will only prolong the struggle and do us no good I fear." She once remarked that she wished "the government would take all we've got and then call out the women and children and see if that would not rouse this people to a sense of their condition."[8]

These were lucid moments which reflected reality. But at times, she did tend to be a bit melodramatic: "There is no pleasure in life and yet we are not willing to die. I do not know how it might be but I feel like I should welcome the *Messenger* if it were not for those who need my services." At another time she complained that "the great trouble is, there is no one on this place that has the welfare and prosperity of the family at heart but me. No one helps me to care and to think. . . . Losses, crosses, disappointments assail me on every hand. Is it because I am so wicked?"[9]

Yet, she was not self-centered. In addition to worrying about her own state of mind, she often thought and wrote of all the people who suffered around her. She might have been speaking for the whole of the district if not for the whole population of the Confederacy in 1864 when she wrote:

> How we pity the brave men who are engaged in these battles. How we sympathize with the anxious hearts which almost stand still with suspense as they turn and listen in every direction for the last scrap of news from the battle. These hearts are more to be pitied than those that lie cold and still on the bloody field. Every body is anxious and gloomy. Constantly we are hearing of some brave man who has fallen and whether an acquaintance or not he is somebody's son, somebody's friend. Some face will grow pale at news of his death, perchance some heart break, some soul pray, in its anguish for death.[10]

As the year 1864 closed, Emily did become increasingly theatrical, yet there was a note of genuine desperation in her comments and a growing sense of self-doubt, a sense that there was something wrong with her. In late 1864 she confronted her depression:

> It is seldom I stop to think of how I feel, much less write about it, but tonight I feel so unnaturally depressed that I cannot help casting about in my mind to see what is the matter. I left home . . . with Mary and Quin . . . to celebrate the anniversary of their marriage. I forgot all I wanted to carry with me. I lost some money. I felt unwell. I came home and found my sick ones not so well, I heard that the troops [with David] . . . were ordered *to sleep with their shoes and cartridge boxes on.* After supper the topic of conversation was Death. Our faithful dog, Boney, has howled ever since dark. What ails me, I do wonder?

Then late one night her husband returned on furlough. "After we all had hugged and kissed our best friend, we raised a light to gaze upon and scrutinize the beloved features which had begun to be something belonging to the past." David looked well and his "arrival has dispelled all gloom for the present."[11] David was well pleased with what Emily had done. By all measures she had managed the farm and the slaves with skill, making enough money and trading wisely enough to live fairly well. From the journal entries during his furlough it is difficult to know if Harris sensed his wife's state of mind. If he did sense the need and the fear, he did not record it, and in two weeks he was once again gone.

David's departure brought on all the old anxieties and fits of depression. Before he could come home again Emily would have to face two new problems, both of which might frighten even the most steadfast personality. By war's end her slaves would grow impudent and rebellious, and desperate men—some soldiers and some deserters—would blanket the countryside. Emily would have to face them both alone.

The war posed special problems for the Harris family and their slaves. The very prospect of war had raised the possibility of slave rebellion in David's mind, and there was one case of alleged planned insurrection in the district in 1860. The fear that war would trigger a slave uprising was general throughout much of the South, but the fears were unfounded. David Harris remained skeptical of the possibility of a general slave uprising in Spartanburg District for much of the war, as we see in this late 1863 description of a sortie prompted by an alleged black conspiracy. A friend came to the house "and warned me to take guns and equipment to repair at dusk to Cedar Spring to watch a big negro-frolick that was to take place. . . . I went according to request (but without my gun) and bravely charged upon the house. But it was dark, silent and quiet, so we charged home again."[12] Otherwise, until the summer of 1864, Harris's relations with his slaves did not change. Every once in a while a slave ran off for a short period, usually because of a flogging, but that was not so unusual.

When David went off to war he was concerned about his wife's ability to manage his slaves. Running the farm was one thing, managing its labor was another. Emily was nervous about the prospect, seemingly without much cause. Then the war turned decidedly sour, and an ominous series of strange events began to plague her. Her field hands began to find hogs butchered on her property. By the summer of 1864 a large number had been killed. At first she believed the culprits might be renegades, but then she was given cause to suspect otherwise. Slaves from the neighborhood had been selling pork for some time, and people were in such need that they did not raise many questions about the source. Also, rumor among her own slaves had it that runaways hiding in the neighborhood were killing her stock. With the help of two neighbors, she interrogated her slaves, but all they could agree upon was that someone else's slave, whose name was Pink, was selling pork. Pink said he had bought the pork from Emily's slave, named Eliphus. She did not believe him and let the matter drop. Emily came to believe that her hogs were being killed "for revenge as well as gain. We have insulted a negro who is too smart to be detected in his villainy."[13] If true, it was the first sign that she might be the object of rebellion.

If the first, this was not the last sign. By 1864, the relationship between masters and slaves was changing in ominous ways. Either because of the news that the war was going badly for the South or because they considered Emily less a master than David, or both, the Harris slaves began to take liberties. At Christmas in 1864 several slaves left the farm without her permission and stayed away at length, and others to whom she had given permission overstayed their time. The same was going on elsewhere in the district. Even more worrisome was a piece of news she learned accidentally, for it showed where the sympathy of these "faithful blacks" lay: "I have learned through negroes that three Yankee prisoners have been living for several days in our gin house and have been fed by our negroes. The neighbors are seen watching for them with their guns." After putting together a surprise raid on her own slave quarters, Emily was disappointed that "the search for Yankee prisoners on our premises ended without success of information except the unmistakeable evidence that some one of more had been lodged and fed in and about our gin for some days. We tried to get the negroes to tell something about it but in vain. We could hear of their telling each other about it, but they wouldn't tell us nothing."[14] The slaves were not rising up, but they were harboring the enemy, and they were keeping things to themselves.

As Emily began to lose control over her slaves, she started to fear them. Many slaves were aware that the Yankees were coming and some began to act on that knowledge, or at least on that hope. In early 1865 "old Will came to me and asked me to give him 'a paper' and let him go and hunt him a home. York [the youngest of the Harris field hands] has given him a whipping and he wishes to leave the place." This was the first request for freedom ever made by a Harris slave. Emily denied it, but the altercation between the two men created a crisis, for Emily was put in a position where she realized the limits of her authority, limits which were an outcome of the times. "I'm in trouble," she wrote; "York must be corrected for fighting the old negro and there is no one willing to do it for me. It seems people are getting afraid of negroes."[15]

The loss of authority hurt in two ways. The district leadership, which before 1861 had sought some justice for African Americans in special courts, was off to war. Wives found that there were severe limits on what they could do to protect their slaves from the irresponsible exercise of power. As many white people grew more fearful of black people late in the war, arbitrary punishments became more frequent and severe. In crises the niceties tend to get trampled. Emily Harris wrote:

NEGRO TRIAL, great trouble. Today some runaway negroes were caught. One of them, Sam, who once belonged to Dr. Dean confessed a good deal and implicated others who were accordingly severely whipped without giving them a chance to probe their innocence. Eliphus [a Harris slave] and Guinn Harris' Pink were both whipped without proof of their guilt. I never will allow another negro of mine punished on suspicion. I understand that on next Monday the const[ables] are to go in search of evidence against Eliphus. Things are reversed. People used to be punished when found guilty, now they are punished and have their trial afterward. Eliphus has cause to deplore the absence of his master as well as I. If he had been here it would not have been managed in this way.[16]

We cannot be certain if Emily let Eliphus know her feelings on the matter, but her indignation was a little late to help him. It is worth noting, however, that she did expect her slave to receive justice.

In 1865, as the weeks of winter and spring passed, Emily lost more and more control over her slaves. She found it "a painful necessity that I am reduced to the use of a stick but the negroes are becoming so impudent and disrespectful that I cannot bear it." In March she set down the plain fact that "the negroes are all expecting to be set free very soon and it causes them to be very troublesome." David Harris reflected a common reaction to the emerging slave attitude when he said, on hearing of an African American who had been shot, that the dead man was "a bad boy & I am glad that he is killed. There is some others in this community that I want to meet the same fate."[17]

The last few months of the war were among the most traumatic for Spartanburg District. When General William T. Sherman captured Savannah in December 1864, South Carolinians realized that he would soon invade their state. They also knew that, as the first Southerners to secede, they were blamed by Union soldiers for the war and that their state stood as a symbol of rebellion. They expected the worst Sherman's army could dish out, and by reputation that could be pretty bad. Knowing that the end was near, some people in the village openly rejoiced at the prospect of peace and even flew a peace flag. There was little adverse reaction even to such a blatant act, for, as Emily put it, "every one seems to think we are to have peace soon and no one seems to care upon what terms." But peace was some months off. Word came to Spartanburg that Sherman was burning Columbia, with thousands of women and children fleeing that part of the state. After hearing about Columbia, Emily Harris described her neighbors and herself as "in a dreadful state of excitement, almost wild. The Yankee army are advancing upon Spartanburg we fear. They are now destroying Alston and Columbia. . . .

It has been impossible for me to sit or be still or do any quiet thing today. I am nearly crazy."[18] Emily had no need to fear, for Sherman turned toward Camden and never came near Spartanburg.

The Union army proved only a distant threat but not so the deserters and renegades who plagued the northern part of the district. These desperadoes became bolder as the Confederate and state forces grew increasingly weak and ineffective. In the middle of 1863, a bad time for the Confederacy in general, the deserters became a serious problem. Their numbers, estimated at anywhere from six hundred to one thousand, were growing and many of them were "armed; are bold, defiant and threatening. Nothing but extreme measures can accomplish anything." So wrote the officer in charge of the Greenville district requesting advice on how to control these marauders. There was even a report that a group of deserters "had fortified an island in the Broad River."[19] The South Carolina troops were detailed to hunt down the deserters, but they were almost bribed into doing so. "By arresting a notorious deserter," David Harris recorded in his journal, "I was granted a twenty days furlough."[20] Most deserters eluded capture largely because they were aided by local citizens who had never been in favor of the war or who were disgusted with it.[21]

By 1864 the deserters and others were getting bolder, stealing food and goods all over Spartanburg District. Food was disappearing from the front yards of farms very close to the village. When Emily Harris heard that a barrel of molasses was stolen from under the bedroom window of her close neighbor, Dr. Dean, she exclaimed of the thieves that "shooting them is the only remedy." Her husband, frustrated by the imminent defeat of the Confederacy, railed at "the thieves about me [who] are troubling me as much as the war. It seems that they will steal all we have got, and leave us but little for my family." By March of 1865 state soldiers who were assigned for local defense despaired of providing adequate protection. One of them wrote to his comrade that "from what I can hear, in the Districts of Union, Spartanburg & Greenville the citizens have been almost overrun by Deserters and absentees from the Army."[22]

The absentees presented a special problem of their own. Throughout the war, the spring had been a time when many men simply walked away from their units. Worried about crops and about their families running out of food, they suffered a special homesickness. In the spring of 1865 all was made worse by the obvious futility of continuing the war, and soldiers set off for home on foot by the thousands. Such a movement of strangers through the district posed problems for Emily Harris: "Late this afternoon a cavalry soldier came and begged to stay all night. I allowed him to stay but shall do so no more. . . . There are hundreds of soldiers passing to and fro. This is a little dangerous for women and children and fine horses to trust themselves on the road." The fear was well founded, but it created pangs of conscience for women who were also loyal citizens and distressed wives. Emily Harris worried that "there are thousands of soldiers now passing through the District on their way to join Gen. Lee near Richmond. Two have just asked to spend the night but I sent them away. In the same way my poor *husband* will be turned away to sleep in the rain and mud."[23] These soldiers were dirty, raggedly dressed, and had not been paid in months. They found themselves thrown onto the mercy of farm and village people who, in turn, felt threatened by these strangers.[24]

Throughout all of her trials—the burden of raising children by herself, managing a farm, handling quarrelsome slaves, and the fear of the dislocation of defeat and the imminence of privation—Emily Harris constantly fought her personal war against depression. More than anything else she feared herself. She believed that her emotions and her mind threatened her world most immediately. In February of 1865, in the midst of rebellious slaves and national defeat, she got the answer to a desperate question she had put to herself months before. "What ails me, I do wonder?" One evening in February she recorded her answer:

A Presentiment

When Mrs. Harris, my esteemed mother in law, among her various objections to her son's alliance with me mentioned that of insanity being an hereditary affliction of my family I laughed at the idea of ever being in any danger of it. But the years which have intervened since then have left upon me the imprint of the trials and sufferings they in passing listered [carved] on me. I sometimes have days of misery for which I cannot give, even to myself, a cause. These spells are periodical and today for the first time I have thought perhaps they were the transitory symptoms of insanity. It is a dark dream to dread. I wonder if the hopelessly insane do suffer much. If it is to be so who can arrest the fate.[25]

Emily Jane Lyles Harris faced the ordeal of increasing slave unrest and the fear of wandering soldiers with the realization that she might be losing her mind. Luckily, her husband came home unhurt within a month. He took over the journal once again, and Emily faded from view, for David hardly mentioned her. However, we do know she did not go insane. Her ordeal stemmed not from insanity, but rather from overwhelming burdens, loneliness, and sensitivity. What is especially striking about her entries in the journal is not that she was depressed, but that her depression made her feel so guilty and incompetent. Indeed, her life gave her ample reason to be fearful and anxious, yet her society expected her to react to her burdens otherwise. Being unable to meet society's expectations, she felt compelled to seek some unnatural explanation, such as her mother-in-law's comment on insanity, for her self-doubts. Emily's anguish stemmed from an unrealistic self-perception fostered in many women during the nineteenth century, a self-perception which even an education by Phoebe Paine could not significantly alter. Emily's reaction to her condition was probably typical of more women, especially farm women, caught up in the Civil War than many people would have us believe. In her remarks about the tedious work, the isolation, and the trouble of daily life, she spoke truly of what much of an antebellum farm existence was like.

David Harris died at age fifty-four in 1875. Emily lived with her children until her death from a stroke suffered, according to family tradition, in a dentist's chair in 1899. The dentist reportedly was badly unsettled by the possibility that he might have brought on the attack. Poor fellow; had he read the journal he would have known that Emily had always had a flair for the dramatic.

7

A Question of Loyalty

I n 1861 Elihu Toland of Glenn Springs published a handbill entitled the "12 We Wonders" under the pseudonym "Brutus." According to court documents read in the 1980s but which are no longer accessible,[1] a farmer named Benjamin Finch believed himself to be one of the targets of this handbill. The publication was distributed among Spartanburg's Confederate troops at the front in Virginia by a cabal of Finch's enemies, among whom was a Dr. Gideon H. King, a resident of Glenn Springs. Finch believed the handbill resulted from rumors that he had restrained his seventeen-year-old son from enlisting. When Elihu Toland, aged 28, returned to Spartanburg from Virginia in 1861, he published another handbill explaining that he had been the person to publish the "12 We Wonders." The two handbills remain among the trial papers concerning the State vs. Benjamin Finch for the murder of Dr. King, aged 60, and they attest to their importance in Finch's defense of his confrontation with Dr. King. The handbills are reprinted in full at the conclusion of this chapter.

On May 9, 1861, the *Carolina Spartan* reported: "Dr. G. H. King, who has been absent for some time on duty in Capt. Kennedy's company of volunteers [Co. K, 3rd Regiment, SCV], has, by petition of the citizens in the neighborhood of Glenn Springs, been honorably discharged by his Excellency Gov. Pickens, that he might return and resume the discharge of his professional duties. The Doctor is again at his post at Glenn Springs." It appears that both Toland and Dr. King returned to Spartanburg at about the same time. The court summoned Toland as a witness in the Finch case. Toland signed a receipt of the summons on January 22, 1862, well after both his return from Virginia and publication of the second handbill, which stated that he was the person to publish the "12 We Wonders." In June 1862, Toland joined the Sixth South Carolina Cavalry for the duration of the war, although he was absent on furlough until November 1862.[2] The court delayed the trial of Benjamin Finch for the duration of the war, and it finally took place in 1866. The trial record showed that Finch met Dr. King on the road at about eight o' clock in the morning and that "on the road King drew and presented a pistol on him [Finch] after getting off his horse . . . and that he (Finch) sprang at the head of King's horse to try to save himself while his gun [Finch was carrying a shot gun] rose and fired and now [after the shooting, Finch] went some distance and turned . . . to see if King was in pursuit . . . [and] saw the horse alone." Finch returned, saw King's body lying in the road, and went off to seek help.[3] No verdict was recorded in the trial papers. On April 12, 1866, the *Carolina Spartan* published the following: "Our Last Court . . . Of the three cases of murder, each of the accused was acquitted. It is a remarkable fact that from so large a number of cases, each should escape the penalty of violated law, but we ascribe it more to the excusable circumstances which accompanied each, than to the want of a proper appreciation of the sense of social obligation

12 We Wonders. Courtesy of the South Carolina Department of Archives and History.

or legal acknowledgment. Certainly none can charge our people with a revenge-ful disposition. Each and every acquittal shows dispassionateness of judgment and coolness of deliberation. The following are the cases alluded to: The State vs. Benjamin Finch." Ultimately Benjamin Finch was found not guilty of murdering Dr. Gideon H. King whom he had blamed for besmirching his character.

The publication of the handbills attests to how seriously some Southerners took loyalty to their new nation. Many of the citizens of the district were con-cerned about the safety and viability of their newly constituted country, a concern that sometimes verged on paranoia, as seen in the *Spartan*'s warnings about pos-sible Union spies and saboteurs in the district. Given that the support in the up-country for secession had been less than total, the supporters of secession seemed ultra patriotic. Dr. King can surely be counted among these, as his service at age sixty early in the war will attest. It would not stretch the imagination to believe that for the supporters of secession, Dr. King was a hero, especially for one such as Toland who, at age 28, joined the cavalry service for the duration of the war. King was the extreme opposite of those persons Toland attacked in the "12 We Wonders."

Toland appears to have felt that anything but total support of the cause was traitorous, and this may have raised his ire enough to make the trouble of produc-ing a handbill for distribution at the front worthwhile. After all, producing the handbill required writing it, having it set in type, and running off many copies. Producing a handbill cost money, time, and considerable effort. It was not a task taken on lightly. Another possibility accounting for the publication of the "12 We Wonders" may be the use of war's circumstances to settle personal or family quarrels. There does not appear to be any evidence of such between Finch and Dr. King, or with Elihu Toland, but the possibility remains. Under these circum-stances the lack of evidence does not indicate a lack of animosity. It appears that we will never know.

From the journal of David Harris and a report in the *Carolina Spartan,* we do know that there was enough pro-Union sentiment in Spartanburg District that Union sympathizers formed themselves into a military unit and drilled publicly. Although this activity did not last long—they disbanded according to Harris, in "fear [of] being hanged"—it is unlikely that the personal feelings of many Unionists changed.[4] The first two of the "12 We Wonders" attests to the agitation that their public actions caused. In the first, Toland suggests that persons with Union sympathies should leave the state, yet he goes one step further. He accuses them of having "abolition" sentiments, a word loaded with connotations attack-ing the foundation of Southern society and likely to inflame the feelings of many

Southerners. Toland made this inference against the background of pro-Union and anti-secession feeling which had been evident in the upper parts of South Carolina for many years, where abolitionism was widely despised. The word "abolitionist" had become an insult used in personal and public attacks that did not necessarily have anything to do with slavery. In an effort to inflame his readers, Toland appropriated it along with all its connotations.

Continuing his attack on the people in the district who did not wholly support secession, Toland then accuses them of the worst of crimes—treason. In this way he declares to his readers that they were now living in a new country, under a new government, all of which was being threatened by an aggressive federal government which had violated their sovereignty by invading them and causing them to go to war. The sentiments of pro-Unionists amounted to treason, the seriousness of which he emphasized by capitalizing its punishment as a "HANGING CRIME."

Only then, in numbers three through nine, does Toland focus his attack on individuals whom he never actually identified. Although he does not give their names, he does describe his targets' unacceptable behavior specifically enough that anyone who had witnessed or heard about it could easily identify them. The specificity of the accusations—sometimes words, sometimes actions, sometimes both—indicate that either Toland knew them personally or knew persons who were acquainted with them. Indeed, it seems unlikely that Toland himself witnessed every one of these seven incidents.

In numbers three through nine Toland describes circumstances that are specific enough to apply to six different men or any combination thereof. There is reason to believe that he refers to separate individuals, for in number four he wrote: "*We wonder* if there is another man (no beast)." The phrase "another man" separated this individual from the person Toland alludes to in number three. Also, in this particular case Toland seems especially angry at the person he is accusing, for he refers to him as a "beast." Although reflecting the nineteenth-century tendency to engage in hyperbole, the characterization seems extreme. Other than numbers six and seven, which Toland said referred to the same person (these appear to be the accusations Finch understood to be aimed specifically at him), all the other accusations seem to refer to separate men, although that is not necessarily the case. Whatever the exact situation, Toland was extremely agitated by these instances of what he considered disloyalty.

Following these personal attacks, Toland once again generalizes his accusations in numbers ten through twelve. The references to "Tories" were inflammatory in resurrecting the animosity shown to those who had refused to join the

Revolutionary cause, helped the British who had invaded South Carolina and occupied her territory, and who patriots believed had fought for a despicable tyranny. Toland's use of the word "Tory" is reminiscent of his earlier use of the word "abolition."

Number twelve is momentarily puzzling. It begins with what seemed to be a question: "*We wonder* if this will fit anybody." But the apparent question was rhetorical for all that preceeds it is meant to answer the question "yes," and the rest of the sentence is a taunt to the person or persons who might have felt attacked by the "*12 We Wonders.*" The last of the final sentence is a challenge posed by Toland to those people who might have tried to discover who had written the handout. The author, in the style of the day, adopted a pseudonym appropriate to the content of the piece. Toland chose to sign the handout, "Brutus," and in so doing raised questions of what was right and just. Brutus had been one of the leaders in ancient Rome who slew the alleged tyrant Julius Caesar. Brutus was descended from a founding family of the Roman Republic, which Brutus believed Caesar was destroying just as Toland believed the federal government was threatening to destroy the republic of the Confederacy.

The existence of the handbills in the trial records of the Finch case is, at least, intriguing. The circumstances which account for the handbills being there remain elusive, except to illustrate the emotion, depth of feeling, and the seriousness of secession and its aftermath even in the country district of Spartanburg.

The "12 We Wonders."

TO THE PUBLIC.

While I was absent from my home, in the service of my country in Virginia, there was certain men, (?) in this District that reported various slanderous *lies* on me; and as I was not present to contradict these lies, they may have gained some credence in the minds of those who do not know me personally.

Now in order to set those things, and myself, right before the people, I will just say that all those *slanderous* reports that went out against me during my absence, were a pack of unmitigated lies—*raised* and *promulgated* by a vile pack of cowardly tories, who had got mad at me because they supposed me to be the author of a certain Handbill, known as the "12 We Wonders,"—which by the way is the only truthful thought they have had lately—and they knew the tales were lies when they raised them, and trotted them around with so much alacrity.

Now I want it to be *expressly* understood, that I consider the *Tory,* who in my absence, tries to ruin my name, no better than the Yankee, who tried to shoot out my heart's blood;—for while I was on the line, enduring the danger and hardships, that no man but a scout endures, with the Yankees's shooting lead at my body, they were at home, enjoying the comforts of their firesides, shooting *lies* at my character.

Now I ask an intelligent people, which is the meanest man the one who shoots lies or lead? I say further, that I wrote the "We Wonders," and will, if necessary, defend them to the last drop of my heart's blood. And all I have to say further concerning this article or the "wonders" is, if either fits *any* man let him *wear it.*

ELIHU TOLAND.

October 20, 1861.[5]

12 WE WONDERS.

1. We *wonder* if this is not the time when men of *Union* (or abolition) sentiments should be getting away from South Carolina?

2. *We wonder* if such men are aware that when they speak in favor of the Union and Abe Lincoln's message and against the Southern Confederacy, that they are committing a HANGING CRIME—treason?

3. *We wonder* if it is possible that a man can be found in Spartanburg District who said he was in hopes all the volunteers who had gone to Virginia or to defend the rights of the Southern Confederacy, would get killed?

4. *We wonder* if there is another man (no beast) who said that he would have been glad if Abe Lincoln's soldiers had been victorious, and killed half of the *secession fools* and villains who retreated from Alexandria, as they did the 'traitor' Jackson?[6]

5. *We wonder* if there is any man in this District so foolish as to believe and be telling 'one-eyed free niggers' that we had three hundred men killed at the battle of Fort Sumter; and we do wonder if that same man did not get that 'news' from that splendid (?) paper he takes, known as the *Brother Jonathan*?

6. *We do wonder* if there is any man in *good circumstances* in this District, who will not let his boys volunteer in defense of their homes, their mothers, sisters and wives, as well as the State and Government which protects him and them?

7. *We wonder* if that same man has given a single dollar to the cause, and if he did not oppose the volunteering of a patriotic young man that was working on his land; and we wonder if he did not talk about turning the widowed mother of that young man off because he had the *patriotism* to volunteer?

8. *We wonder* if there is any body in Spartanburg who said, the day of the election for members to the convention last December, that if there was

any glory in voting for secession that others might have it, that he 'did not want any of it?'

9. *We wonder* if there is not a man in this District that bought two Colt's rifles, and paid $76 for them, and bought to keep the secessionists from shipping for being a 'sub.,' and now when he counts up what he has done for his country, he always puts in the rifles at $76, and one $1 that he paid for the support of a man's wife, that is going to fight for him and his property?

10. *We wonder* if there is any man or family in this District that is not represented in this, the contest for liberty; and we wonder if they can *enjoy* the 'liberty' well after it is obtained.

11. *We wonder* if such men won't feel something like the *Tories* did after the revolution of '76; and if they won't be remembered with as much fondness as they were and are yet?

12. *We wonder* if this *will* fit any body, and if so, if they won't want the man's name that wrote it, and if they do, if they can't get it?

BRUTUS[7]

8

Having Fled War

As soon as war broke out the coastal areas of the Confederacy became vulnerable to Union attack. President Abraham Lincoln determined early on to blockade the Southern coast which was over 3000 miles long. Even as the Northern navy grew and the blockade became increasingly effective, it could never truly prevent all shipping from Southern ports. The South Carolina coast was subject to invasion because of all the rivers and marshes that covered it, and as early as 1861 federal troops occupied an area around Port Royal. As the war wore on Union troops increased their raids on plantations along the coast and laid siege to Charleston. Many Southerners with coastal plantations abandoned them, for the Confederacy was unable to spare the manpower needed to prevent Northern attacks.

These Southerners often sought refuge inland and tried to save as much of their property as they could, especially their slaves. Areas around Camden, Aiken, Columbia, Chester, and other midland towns were the preferred choices for temporary quarters. Eventually, however, the number of refugees grew so large that people had to look to the towns of the upcountry. As one of these towns, Spartanburg also collected its population of lowcountry refugees. It was a desperate choice for many people. As one refugee said of another: "She is at the Walker House with her daughters[;] they find it not nice, every one complains. Most people stay a few days and then locate themselves."[1] Locating themselves might mean buying a house, but even then refugees were not always satisfied. One Spartanburg District resident wrote her brother: "Some of the Refugees are very much dissatisfied in Spartanburg. [They] Think the country people might put up with any and every privation for them."[2]

For many village dwellers providing daily needs could be difficult, but for William Kennedy Blake, one of the inhabitants who took in refugees, it was almost impossible.[3] Blake had become a fixture in the community soon after taking the presidency of the Spartanburg Female College in 1859. The war, ironically, proved a short term blessing for his school. Many lowcountry people seeking a haven from the threat of federal troops considered Spartanburg isolated enough yet adequately civilized to be a place of refuge. Also, many lowcountry planters sent their daughters to the Spartanburg Female College to get them away from the danger of federal invasion, and so during the early period of the war the institution flourished. However with over one hundred people to feed as times grew very hard Blake had his hands full. As the Confederate money he had received in tuition became increasingly worthless he had to resort to barter and begging. Luckily his wife was a niece of William Gregg, who owned the textile mill at Graniteville, and the prominent manufacturer gave Blake a great deal of cloth which he used as a means of exchange. He describes one of his foraging trips:

> For years it was my practice on Saturday morning to mount my saddle horse and proceed to the country on a foraging expedition. My two horse wagon and driver would follow with instructions to stop at certain places and take up the supplies that I might be able to buy. Sometimes I would get full rations for a week, but not infrequently the supply was so limited that I would not know how or from where the next day's meal was to be provided; some days I would have two or three beeves hanging in my smokehouse and again there would not be scraps of meat on the premises to get up a hash.

Yet, in the face of adversity, there was little complaint as "old and young appreciated the situation." Blake indicates that there existed a camaraderie at the school and that everyone bore up well together. His view is corroborated in a letter by one of his pupils, Anna Donaldson, written to her parents in 1863 in which she said she was "very well pleased with everything here. . . . Mr. Blake had kept a very nice room for us over his room, on the second floor. It contains two beds[,] table and glass[,] and washstand. We have five in the room now. . . . The school is very full. I do not know the exact number, something over a hundred. Mr. Blake has refused to receive any more. Some rooms have as many as seven girls in them. The school is said to be flourishing [more] than it has been for years." Conditions were crowded, but the overcrowding did not seem to bother the refugees. The girls were content largely because Blake made the school an interesting place to be. Anna Donaldson continued: "I like Mr. Blake very much, he is so kind to the girls, and takes a great deal of pains to make us understand our lessons. . . . The fare is good enough. We have bread and beef for breakfast very well seasoned, the same with potatoes, and sometimes cabbage for dinner, and bread and molasses for supper. Mr. Blake says it is not his fault that we have nothing better to eat, people will not let him have provisions for love nor money. He asks most every one who brings daughters here if they cannot spare him something to eat."[4]

The problems at the school were compounded by the presence of several adult refugees that Blake also took in. The refugees paid him for sheltering them, some in cash which became increasingly useless, and others in goods or labor. One of the refugees brought about fifteen slaves with her which Blake used about the college or rented out in the district. Hers was not an unusual case, for many of the people who came to Spartanburg from other parts of the state brought their slaves with them. Slaves were the most mobile of all a planter's heavy investments, and masters endeavored to keep their slaves out of the hands of the Union forces. The village benefited from the many refugees, for they lent it a somewhat more cosmopolitan air, but their presence in the already overburdened district added to the drain on local resources. In addition, the refugees had their own special difficulties in adjusting to the rural existence that constituted life in Spartanburg village.

One of the most distinguished families to seek refuge in Spartanburg was the Grimballs who came from an area in Colleton District, now part of Charleston County. John and his wife, Margaret Ann "Meta" Grimball, were both wealthy; Meta was the daughter of a rich New Yorker who had married a Manigault of Charleston, and John owned two lowcountry plantations. Grimball valued his 1560 acres at $57,000 [$1,540,000] and his 143 slaves at $78,000 [$2,110,000].[5] The Grimballs had six sons and three daughters. In 1862 Meta wrote in her journal: "We are now in a great state of excitement, all the lowcountry getting into the upper country. Flying from our Ruthless foes, we expect an attack and people are leaving their houses and families servants and furniture, crowding up to the Rail Road. The upper districts are crowded with this unusual population and food is not abundant or cheap. The people in many instances take advantage of this state of things and put a great price on their houses refusing to rent but choosing to sell. . . . We are now trying in Spartanburg."[6]

After trying to rent property in other parts of the upper districts, John Grimball succeeded in renting rooms in Spartanburg village where he paid forty dollars ($895) per month for the east wing of St. John's College. The family arrived in a private railroad car in June of 1862. They expected to stay a few months; at the very most a year. As with many other Southerners, the Grimballs had no idea that the war would last so long.[7]

The family moved into the east wing of St. John's College, located on the present site of Converse College. They had seven rooms, three upstairs and three downstairs, plus a very large room which they divided with screens into a pantry, a dining room, and a drawing room.[8] Meta Grimball was totally in charge of her new home. She shouldered the responsibility for it and for her family because her husband was normally away from the village on business. Shortly before leaving the Lowcountry, Meta began a journal which she kept throughout her experience in Spartanburg. From it we can see the village and its people in wartime from the perspective of an aristocratic planter's wife who had been comfortably at home in the social and political whirl that characterized the antebellum life of the much vaunted plantation society of the lowcountry.

Meta Grimball considered herself lucky to have her lodgings at forty dollars. Many of her friends, on first coming to Spartanburg, lodged at the Walker house, but finding accommodations there not good—the food bad and the rooms mean—they paid dearly for anything elsewhere in the district. Meta's father-in-law, an irascible old man, came up to live with her when his plantations were threatened. He was difficult; embittered by having to leave his beautiful home, he became quick tempered and hard to please. The village was soon made aware of his presence when he became irate at the vestry of Spartanburg's Episcopal Church for not allowing a lowcountry preacher to use their pulpit. Their reason was that the priest was a Yankee, and it was only after Mr. Grimball made considerable fuss that the priest was able to preach a little. The Grimballs believed the upcountry people were rather narrow-minded and inflexible.

Meta Grimball found the quiet life of the village uncomfortable. There seemed nothing to do and the days were so long. "The only way to get along," she decided, "is to earnestly pursue a daily routine, & hope for the best and enjoy all that comes in ones way & be thankful." To combat the depression which accompanied her sense of isolation, Meta entered into what passed for social life in the village. As a well-educated, aristocratic woman she was immediately sought out by Spartanburg society. At home she organized her family into a routine of sewing, gaming, and schooling, for her children also missed the hubbub that had once filled their lives. Yet the isolated feeling was always present. When Meta heard a rumor, which turned out to be false, that the railroad was to be torn up to mend other roads, she panicked. "I don't know how we are to get away or hear of the outer world," she wrote, "for the horses are all taken up by the Army and there will be no Stage or mail more than . . . [once] or twice a week."

With eligible daughters and sons in the house it was almost inevitable that the Grimballs' lives would become fuller. Their wide-ranging contact with Spartanburg society gave Meta a chance to compare village society with that of the lowcountry. She often engaged visitors in long conversations about the habits and lives of the upcountry people. To her everyone in the district, whether on a farm or in the village, was "country," but it was evident to her that village people distinguished between farm and town people. From a long conversation with Whitefoord Smith, the president of St. John's College, she recorded a comment which revealed not only a common view of farm folk but a keen insight into a little acknowledged result of the war:

> Dr. Smith thinks the war will be a great benefit to the country, for it will provide an enlargement of mind to very ignorant, contracted, country people. The families of soldiers now take newspapers, and if they can't read themselves they get people to read to them, and some of them have learned to read themselves. One woman in his neighborhood whose husband, a hard working man and gone off to the wars, had learnt to write & read writing since her husband left her, and he had, too, learned to read & write that he might write to her, she could read his letters, but no other writing.

Mrs. Grimball very much appreciated Smith and enjoyed his visits, as well she might. But she was somewhat puzzled by village society. It appeared to her that there was no acknowledged group, no class which carried the burden of setting an example for the rest to follow. In the lowcountry the large plantation owners were at the pinnacle of society, and the lives they led were often acknowledged as worthy of emulation. Meta was somewhat shocked to find Spartanburg "a district of a low character in Morals. I do not hear of anyone being more correct than another." Such a democratic character was not to her liking; the lack of deference and the informality made her uncomfortable. She once visited a woman of standing in the community in the lady's bed chamber where she was entertaining her guests: "Mrs. L's husband came for her, walking in the chamber with out knocking. He is a Tailor, so we found ourselves in rather unusual company. In a village there is not distinction, all meet on an equality, and consequently the manners of these people are . . . rather more alike than is usually found." In some ways Meta Grimball felt more comfortable and at ease in the intimate company of her servants than in the company of villagers. She lovingly described a scene where her boys "sat at the fire with their old Mauma [a slave]. W[illiam] smoking and the old Mauma smoking too; quite comfortably & having a cozy talk."

Such a response on Meta's part should not be surprising, for class distinctions had been acknowledged in the South since the seventeeth century. Perhaps no section of the country had maintained its adherence to social class distinctions as predominantly as the Southern states, and within that region none so much as South Carolina. The South had been influenced less than the rest of the nation by the Jacksonian revolution—which had stressed equality over wealth and social

James Bivings, an early pioneer of cotton mills in the district, built this mansion on the village's northern border in 1856. Photograph courtesy of the Herald-Journal Willis Collection, Spartanburg County, South Carolina, Public Libraries.

rank—ironic though this may seem as Jackson had been a Southern slave holder. Spartanburg District, with its paucity of large plantations, ostentatious planters' homes, and only a relatively rural and unimpressive district center, had an equality amongst its residents uncharacteristic of the middle and lowcountry regions of South Carolina. Meta's remark that "In a village there is not distinction, all meet on an equality" was true by lowcountry standards, though by upcountry standards not quite as absolute as she made it sound.

The Grimballs had difficulty getting supplies and had to pay very high prices for them. Finding enough food for a large family and servants was a constant job, and later in the war when the family plantations were shut down the Grimballs began to run out of money. The Grimballs were wealthy and by the time their money ran short most other refugees had already had to cope with severe want. An informal society emerged amongst the refugees, for they all shared common problems that set them apart from the natives in the village. Anytime that a refugee family or any of their village friends received a special treat or made a lucky purchase in the District they went out of their way to share their good luck.

Coming from the lowcountry and being known as wealthy proved a handicap in some ways. People in the village took for granted that the Grimballs were not in need, and that they would be eager to make good business deals. Many local people who had anything to sell turned to Meta as a likely buyer, a practice that led her to remark that "a great deal of property is offered for sale and changes hands at very high prices, negroes particularly." Indeed, during the last months of the war advertisements of the sale of slaves appeared more and more frequently in the pages of the *Carolina Spartan*. As each of these sales usually appeared only once or twice there seemed to be a sufficient number of purchasers. The Grimballs' supposed wealth sometimes proved an embarrassment: "two poor women recently came here to beg. I was not able to give them meal, for I find it hard to get it for my own family, and had no change: but this morning when I was in the Village I passed one of them & gave her 25 c having felt badly at refusing her all aid, when she applyed to me at the door." This incident occurred in 1862; three years later, in late 1865, Meta was less understanding, made so by her own trials and hardships: "Two women very decently dressed have come here twice, not to beg, but to borrow money: the old one was so fierce looking. I dreaded her curses and she asked for $2, so I *lent* her one, and the girl 50c, it seems to me it may be a good way of getting rid of these Spartanburg beggars."

The Grimballs lost their eldest son, a physician, in the war, with the loss eased somewhat by the presence of his father at his deathbed. One of the daughters went to teach in the nearby town of Union, and the other two opened a small school in Spartanburg, all in 1864. The girls were independently minded and took these positions against their mother's wishes. The money helped out, but in the spring of 1865, circumstances forced the girls to refuse payment in Confederate money and instead request payment in goods, such as food and clothing, valued at pre-war prices. A bit earlier, Meta Grimball had written in her journal that she had "no heart to write a journal now. The war goes on but so much distress and suffering. Charleston evacuated, Columbia sacked & burned, Cheraw, Winnsborough, Camden, Society Hill & other places visited by the Army of Sherman & sacked and burned. . . . Harry received an appointment from the Governor. . . . This has been a great trial to me for he is the youngest and not yet sixteen. I fear all the fatigue & hardship he will not be able to stand; and my heart yearns over this child." It was small comfort for Meta Grimball to know that she was not alone in her anxiety.

It had been an unusually wet season in that spring of 1865, and all was lush green about St. John's College, when John Berkly Grimball sat at his writing desk, listening to the falling rain. In true nineteenth century fashion, the weather seemed to reflect the mood of this temporary visitor to the Upstate, whose stay had marked the loss of his fortune, his hopes for his country, and his way of life. And on that wet and bleak day, John Berkly Grimball knew that the presence of the Yankees in the village had brought home the truth, and he wrote: "We are beginning to realize that we are a conquered people."[9]

Conclusion

War had not been the short-lived, adventurous, and triumphant experience almost everyone in Spartanburg had expected—not for the soldier in the field, and not for the people at home. Instead, it had necessitated unexpected sacrifice and caused social turmoil—it had proven hard and unforgiving. So it was for the Confederate and the border states, and so it was for the people of Spartanburg. Geographically removed from the terrors of the battlefields, the people of Spartanburg had experienced the war in their own ways. They had experienced the hardship of high taxes and the scarcity of food, the worry of having sons, husbands, and friends subject to the maiming and death of war, the tension of political bickering and bitter disagreements among leaders and neighbors, the fear of possible depredations from returning soldiers and deserters, and for many, the depression of lost hope and the longing for peace followed by the finality of the end of nationhood. For Spartanburg's slaves, the war had meant sharing much or even more of the above as well as enduring the uncertainty between continued slavery or obtaining freedom. The end of the war had seemed to fulfill the hopes of Spartanburg's slaves, but for the white people who had initially been caught up in the romance and excitement of rebellion and independence, it meant the bitterness of defeat.

In the end the self-proclaimed greatest society the world had ever known had for the most part ceased to be. Insofar as the Southern way of life had depended on slavery, whether one had owned slaves or had aspired to doing so, that way of life was forever destroyed. As the subsequent history of the white people of the Southern region, including the residents of Spartanburg, would show, the defeat of the battlefield did not mean that they had changed their minds in any fundamental ways. As John Berkly Grimball wrote, they had been "conquered," but as their subsequent actions would attest, they had not been reconstructed.

Ironically, the "fifth column" the *Spartan* had so often feared in its pages during the war became, at war's end, the posture of many white Spartanburg residents.[1]

The fighting war was over, but the cultural battle would continue over one hundred more years, and may yet not be finished. Perhaps, for all the residents of Spartanburg whose lives were touched by war, it is fitting to leave the last word to two of the Union generals who ultimately defeated them. Ulysses S. Grant wrote of those Southern fighting men: "I felt like anything rather than rejoicing at the downfall of a foe who had fought so long and valiantly, and had suffered so much for a cause."[2] William Tecumseh Sherman wrote: "we are not only fighting hostile armies, but a hostile people, and must make old and young, rich and poor, feel the hard hand of war, as well as their organized armies."[3] In both instances the words of these two magnanimous and victorious warriors aptly apply to the war-time experiences of the inhabitants of Spartanburg District.

NOTES

Chapter One: The Setting

1. Works Progress Administration, *A History of Spartanburg County, American Guide Series* (1940; Spartanburg, S.C.: The Reprint Company, 1976), 37. Also see Doyle Boggs, *Historic Spartanburg County: 225 Years of History* (Spartanburg, S.C.: Spartanburg County Historical Association, 2012), 9.

2. *Carolina Spartan* (Spartanburg, S.C.), 10 April 1851, 29 June 1854.

3. 1860 United States Census.

4. For an example of one who purchased bonds late in the war see Philip N. Racine, *Gentlemen Merchants: A Charleston Family's Odyssey, 1828–1870* (Knoxville: University of Tennessee Press, 2008), 721; David L. Carlton, *Mill and Town in South Carolina 1880–1920* (Baton Rouge: Louisiana University Press, 1982), chapters 1 and 2.

5. Philip N. Racine, ed., *Piedmont Farmer: The Journals of David Golightly Harris, 1855–1870* (Knoxville: University of Tennessee Press, 1986). For various attempts see index.

6. Sarah Cudd Gaskins, "The Pioneer Church as an Agency of Social Control: An Analysis of the Record of Two Baptist Churches in South Carolina from 1803–1865 Inclusive," Master's thesis, University of Pittsburg, 1936; Albert J. Raboteau, *Slave Religion: The "Invisible Institution" in the Antebellum South* (New York: Oxford University Press, 2004).

7. William Joseph MacArthur, "Antebellum Politics in an Upcountry County, National, State, and Local Issues in Spartanburg County, South Carolina, 1850–1860," Masters thesis, University of South Carolina, 1966, 5–6. I did most of my research on the following political matters many years ago, and much of what I found is in agreement with and was subsequently published by Bruce Eelman in his *Entrepreneurs in the Southern Upcountry* (Athens: University of Georgia Press, 2008), chapts. 1 and 2. My major disagreement with Eelman is that he connects political activities too closely with economic issues; although I do agree that economic factors were important, I believe there were more nuanced causes.

8. *Carolina Spartan,* 13 March 1849.

9. Henry to S. F. Patterson, 8 August 1849, Samuel Finley Patterson Papers, Duke University Library, Special Collections Library Research Room.

10. Eelman, *Entrepreneurs,* 16–19.

11. See chapter eight.

12. Racine, *Piedmont,* 63.

Chapter Two: Spartanburg Wages War

1. Racine, *Piedmont,* 171; for the episode of the Union company, see 174 and 178.

2. James T. Otten, "Disloyalty in the Upper Districts of South Carolina during the Civil War," *South Carolina Historical Magazine,* 75, (April, 1974): 95–110.

3. For these districts, see Frank A. Dickson, J*ourneys into the Past: The Anderson Region's Heritage* (N.p.: 1975), 125–36; Archie Vernon Huff, Jr., *Greenville: The History of the City and County in the South Carolina Piedmont* (Columbia: University of South Carolina Press, 1995), chapter 5; R. W. Simpson, *History of Old Pendleton District. . . .* (Greenville, S.C.: Southern Historical Press, 1978), 39–44.

4. Racine, *Piedmont,* 190.

5. Ibid., 203.

6. Ibid., 205.

7. For patrol and fire watch, see Spartanburg City Council Minutes, 21 December 1860; on collecting arms, see 14 June 1861. For the iron works see Charles E. Cauthen, ed., *Journals of the South Carolina Executive Councils of 1861 and 1862* (Columbia: University of South Carolina Press, 1956), 19 February 1862.

8. *Carolina Spartan,* 26 September 1861.

9. On insurrection see Racine, *Piedmont,* 182. For an example of an interrogation, see Spartanburg City Council Minutes, 17 July 1863.

10. William Kennedy Blake, "Recollections," Southern Historical Collection, University of North Carolina, 80–81.

11. Reidville, June 24, 1861 (Andrew Pickens, Official Correspondence, 1860–1862. South Carolina Department of Archives and History): ST 1688.

12. Marcus H. Wall, Jr., "Spartanburg District, Confederate Troops 1861–1865 According to Dr. J. B. O. Landrum" (n.p., 1997).

13. *Carolina Spartan,* 2 June 1864.

14. *Ibid.,* 28 July 1864.

15. For comments of students volunteering, see Christopher Smith to Minnie and Mary Smith, 18 April 1861, Elihu Penquite Smith Papers, South Caroliniana Library, University of South Carolina; on Col. Edward's Regiment, see Major T. Stobo Farrow to Francis W. Pickens, [1861], Thomas Stobo Farrow Papers, South Caroliniana Library, University of South Carolina. A troop of cavalry formed as early as 28 January 1861, see South Carolina Statutes, no. 4519, 1861.

16. On drilling, see Racine, *Piedmont,* 179; on Charleston, see 190.

17. Smith to mother, 7 June 1861, Smith Papers.

18. Smith to sister, 9 August 1861, Smith Papers.

19. Stephen Moore to his wife, Rachel, 8 July 1862, in Tom Moore Craig, ed., *Upcountry South Carolina Goes to War: Letters of the Anderson, Brockman, and Moore Families 1853–1865* (Columbia: University of South Carolina Press), 97.

20. Eliphas Smith to mother, 4 November 1861, Smith Papers.

21. Eliphas Smith to mother, 13 December 1861, Smith Papers; also see T. J. Moore to Thomas W. Hill, 17 July 1862, Thomas John Moore Papers, South Caroliniana Library, University of South Carolina.

22. Frank E. Vandiver, *Their Tattered Flags* (New York: Harper & Row, 1970), 129–31.

23. The course of these events is described in Racine, *Piedmont,* 245–53; quotations are on 252–53.

24. Charles Edward Cauthen, *South Carolina Goes to War 1860–1865* (Chapel Hill: University of North Carolina Press, 1950), 138.

25. Racine, *Piedmont,* 266.

26. T. J. Moore to T. W. Hill, 29 April 1863, in Craig, *Upcountry South Carolina,* 119.

27. "Minutes," Spartanburg Methodist Sunday School Relief Society, 1861–1863, Thomas D. Johnson Papers, Southern Historical Collection, University of North Carolina. The following account is taken from these minutes.

28. *Carolina Spartan,* 29 August 1861.

29. Memminger to Whitefoord Smith, 5 October 1861, Whitefoord Smith Papers, Duke University Library, Special Collections Library Research Room.

30. *Carolina Spartan,* 21 August 1861. For other such groups see the *Carolina Spartan* for 29 August 1861 which mentions such an association in Cedar Spring. There are various such reports scattered in the *Spartan* throughout the war years.

31. *Ibid.,* 5 September 1861.

32. "Broadside," Amateur Concert, 23 September 1861, Ladies Relief Association, Spartanburg, South Caroliniana Library, University of South Carolina.

33. Walker to Mrs. H. J. Dean, 11 August 1862, Simpson,Young Papers, South Caroliniana Library, University of South Carolina.

34. For hospitals, see *Margaret Ann Morris Grimball Diary, 1860–1866,* 10 October 1862, Southern Historical Collection, University of North Carolina; for individuals, see Blake, "Recollections," 81.

35. *Carolina Spartan,* 14 July 1864.

36. Margaret Ann Morris Grimball Diary, 5 September 1862.

37. Ibid., 7 September 1862.

38. Smith to wife, 2 July 1862, Smith Papers.

39. Grimball Diary, 7 September 1862. All three young men had been students together at Wofford College; see David Duncan Wallace, *History of Wofford College 1854–1949* (Nashville: Vanderbilt University Press, 1951), 72.

40. James Farrow to John L. Manning, 30 October 1862, Chesnut-Miller-Manning Papers, South Carolina Historical Society.

41. For revocation of permits see Charles E. Cauthen, ed., *Journals of the South Carolina Executive Councils of 1861 and 1862* (Columbia: University of South Carolina Press, 1956), 287; for legislative action see S. C. Statutes, no. 4629, 18 December 1862.

42. South Carolina Statutes, no. 4671, 1863, and no. 4701, 1864. On the tax in kind, see *Carolina Spartan,* 3 May 1864.

43. *Carolina Spartan*, 3 May 1864

44. Ibid, 16 June 1864.

Chapter Three: Spartanburg Beleaguered

1. For a full discussion of cotton see Vandiver, *Tattered Flags*, 88–89, 101; "Lincolnite" comment is in Racine, *Piedmont*, 213; the order to overseer is in A. C. Moore to Nancy Moore, 1 February 1862, Moore Papers.

2. J. B. O. Landrum, *History of Spartanburg County*. . . . 1900; rpt., (Spartanburg, S.C.: The Reprint Company, 1985), 513.

3. Ibid., 664–722.

4. Racine, *Piedmont*, 243.

5. *Carolina Spartan*, 26 February 1863.

6. The starvation comment is in Racine, *Piedmont*, 252; the lament on crops, 254.

7. Ibid., 246 and 251.

8. *Carolina Spartan*, 5 November 1863.

9. The amounts within the parentheses are conversions to what these amounts would be worth in 2010 using the Consumer Price Index. These are rough estimations as money was so badly inflated in the Confederacy. On the other hand it does give some idea of the values being discussed. Samuel H. Williamson, "Seven Ways to Compute the Relative Value of a U.S. Dollar Amount, 1774 to present," MeasuringWorth, April 2010, http://www.measuringworth.com/ppowerus/.

10. Racine, *Piedmont*, 290.

11. The fancy remark is in Racine, *Piedmont*, 303; the Ben Finch remark is on 363.

12. *Carolina Spartan*, 6 November 1862.

13. Ibid., 21 April 1864.

14. See Ibid. 23 January 1862 and 3 December 1863.

15. Racine, *Piedmont*, 286.

16. *Carolina Spartan*, 23 June 1864.

17. Smith to E. Smith, 6 August 1863, Smith Papers.

18. For a similar discussion of this issue, see Eelman, *Entrepreneurs*, 129–30.

19. Racine, *Piedmont*, 239, 326.

20. Ibid., on outlaws see 349, 346, 353, 375, 377; on butchered livestock see 333, 353; warnings about permitting soldiers to spend night, 366.

21. Ibid., 236.

22. Ibid., 302.

23. *Carolina Spartan*, 3 September 1863.

24. Ibid.

25. Vandiver, *Tattered Flags*, 265–67.

26. Eliphas Smith to mother, 6 October 1863, Smith Papers.

27. Quotations in Racine, *Piedmont*, 311, 317 and 319.

28. Andrew C. Magrath to Col. I. B. Palmer, 27 February 1865, Andrew C. Magrath Papers, Letters Received and Sent, 1865, South Carolina Department of Archives and History.

29. Racine, *Piedmont,* 369.

30. Blake, "Recollections."

Chapter Four: Slavery during the War

1. 1860 Census and 1860 Slave Census of Spartanburg District.

2. Racine, *Piedmont,* 182.

3. Ibid., 314.

4. Ibid., on hogs see 333 and 353; on her belief in "the guilt of a Negro" see 351; on impudence and the beating of slaves, see 365; on expectations of freedom, see 367; on harboring Yankee escapees, see 353–54; on fearing slaves, see 357–58.

5. Ibid., 351.

6. Spartanburg Magistrates and Freeholders Court Records, Case No. 231, South Carolina Department of Archives and History.

7. For gambling see Statutes, no. 2639, 1834; for the oath see City Council Minutes, 20 February 1837.

8. City Council Minutes, 19 January 1853.

9. Ibid., 31 January 1853 and 22 October 1859.

10. *Carolina Spartan,* 5 March 1857.

11. For hiring out practices and campaigns to ban blacks from trades, see Michael Johnson and James L. Roark, *Black Masters: A Free Family of Color in the Old South* (Boston: W. W. Norton, 1986), and Richard Wade, *Slavery in the Cities: The South 1820–1860* (New York: Oxford University Press), 1967.

12. On passes see City Council Minutes, 7 May 1853.

13. Ibid.

14. *Carolina Spartan,* 16 July 1857.

15. City Council Minutes, 16 May 1857.

16. For appeals that were successful much to the chagrin of Spartanburg's whites see Philip N. Racine, "The Trials and Tribulations of Jesse Hughey, Free Negro," *The Proceedings of the South Carolina Historical Association,* 1985: 29–39.

17. Sparanburg District Magistrates and Freeholders' Court, 1824–1856. South Carolina Departmnet of Archives and History.

18. For a fuller analysis of this court see Philip N. Racine, "The Spartanburg District Magistrates and Freeholders Court, 1824–1865," *South Carolina Historical Magazine,* 87 (October 1986): 197–212.

19. Case no. 184 (1856), Freeholders' Court.

20. Case no. 97 (1849), ibid.

21. Case no. 88 (1848), ibid.

22. Case no. 160 (1854), ibid.

23. Case no. 105 (1849), ibid.

24. Case no. 218 (1858), ibid.

25. Case no. 231 (1860), ibid.

26. On jailing see City Council Minutes, 17 October 1860. For a state law on passes see Statutes, no. 4501, 1861.

27. City Council Minutes, 6 February 1861.

28. *Carolina Spartan*, 21 April 1864.

29. Meta Morris Grimball, Diary, January 1865, Southern Historical Collection, University of North Carolina.

30. Case no. 278 (1864), Freeholders' Court.

31. For a fuller view of violence among slaves see Jeff Forret, "Conflict and the 'Slave Community': Violence among Slaves in Upcountry South Carolina," *The Journal of Southern History* 74, no. 3 (2008): 551–88.

32. Case no. 271 (1864), Freeholders' Court.

33. Freeholder's Court.

34. Case no. 276 (1864), ibid.

35. Case no. 302 (1865), ibid.

Chapter Five: The Slave Catherine and the Kindness of Strangers?

Reprinted in slightly altered form from Philip N. Racine, "The Slave Catherine and the Kindness of Strangers," *South Carolina Historical Magazine*, 113, (April 2012).

1. Andrew Magrath's Papers, Letters Received and Sent, 1865, South Carolina Department of Archives and History, folder 25.

2. Ibid.

3. Trial Record, folder 25, Magrath Papers.

4. Ibid.

5. Ibid., folder 33.

6. Petition to Gov. Magrath, folder 25, Magrath Papers.

7. United States Census, Spartanburg, South Carolina, 1860 and the United States Slave Census, Spartanburg, South Carolina, 1860.

8. Assuming her prosecutor, Davis Moore, was also responsible for her incarceration, his signature on the petition indicated his distress at her plight which was translated into action as he permitted a minister to see her often.

9. Information was gathered from the United States, South Carolina, Spartanburg, 1860 Population Census, the 1850 and 1860 Slave Schedules and J. B. O. Landrum's, *Spartanburg County.*

10. O'Neall, John Belton, *The Negro Law of South Carolina, collected and Digested by John Belton O'Neall, One of the Judges of the Courts of Law and Errors of the Said State. . . .* (Columbia: State Agricultural Society of South Carolina, 1848).

11. "An Act for the Better Ordering and Governing Negroes and Other Slaves of This Province" (1740), South Carolina Statutes, 397, no. 670.

12. Ibid, 399, Section 6.

13. Ibid., 412, Sec. 39.

14. O'Neall, *Negro Law*, 18, Sec. 11.

15. Ibid., 19, Sec. 19.

16. Ibid., 20, Sec. 24.

17. Ibid, 21, Sec. 27.

18. Ibid., 20, Sec. 20.

Chapter Six: Emily Lyles Harris: Reluctant Farmer

Reprinted in slightly altered form with permission from Philip N. Racine, "Emily Lyles Harris: A Piedmont Farmer During the Civil War." *South Atlantic Quarterly*, 79 (1980): 386-97.

1. Reminiscence of Mrs. Laura L. Harris, typescript in private hands. Unless otherwise noted all quotations in this chapter are from Racine, *Piedmont*.

2. In July 1862 David suffered from severe headaches; Racine, *Piedmont*, 344–45.

3. Emily Liles Harris, Journals. Special Collections, Dacus Library, Winthrop University, 18 November 1862.

4. Racine, *Piedmont, 268.*

5. Ibid., 269–70.

6. Unfortunately the letters written to one another are not extant.

7. Racine, *Piedmont*, 275, 309, 335.

8. Ibid., 310, 332, 358, 361.

9. Ibid., 340, 343.

10. Ibid., 331.

11. Ibid., 345, 347.

12. Ibid., 314.

13. Ibid., 353–54.

14. Ibid.

15. Ibid., 357–58.

16. Ibid., 360.

17. Ibid., 365, 367, 369.

18. Ibid., 363, 364–65.

19. Otten, "Disloyalty," 102.

20. Racine, *Piedmont*, 311.

21. John Durant Ashmore to [unknown], Greenville, S.C., 30 August 1863, John Durant Ashmore Papers, South Caroliniana Library, University of South Carolina.

22. Racine, *Piedmont*, 346, 348–49; J. A. Keller to Col. John M. Obey, 16 March 1865, J. A. Keller Papers, South Caroliniana Library, University of South Carolina.

23. On reading this entry, one Southern veteran of the Vietnam War commented that Emily was lucky her barn was not burned to the ground.

24. Racine, *Piedmont, 370.*

25. Ibid., 364. Emily's maternal grandparents were first cousins, which may have been what her mother-in-law objected to.

Chapter Seven: A Question of Loyalty

1. I read the full trial record in the 1980's while doing research on my edition of the Harris Journals (Racine, *Piedmont*) and took full notes on the incident since David Harris ended up serving as a character witness for Benjamin Finch and also on the jury. For this book I sought to reread these records only to find all but the two handbills missing.

2. Toland joined for duty and enrolled in the 6th South Carolina Cavalry as a private under Capt. James Knight's Company E in Aiken's Regiment, Partisan Rangers and was

mustered in at Camp Preston on 21 July 1862. Service Records, C2922, South Carolina Department of Archives and History.

3. Court of General Sessions, Spartanburg County, State of South Carolina, South Carolina Department of Archives and History.

4. Racine, *Piedmont,* 173–74.

5. "To the public: Elisha Toland Oct. 20, 1861" Spartanburg Court of General Sessions Benjamin Finch 1866 #6, South Carolina Department of Archives and History.

6. Toland is referring to the threat made by President Andrew Jackson during the nullification crisis to use force to crush South Carolina's attempt to interpose itself between the federal government and the citizens of the state. Until that time, Jackson, a slave holder, had been considered a friend of the South.

7. "12 We Wonders," signed Brutus, Spartanburg Court of General Sessions, Benjamin Finch 1866 #6 Broadside, South Carolina Department of Archives and History.

Chapter Eight: Having Fled War

1. Margaret Ann Morris Grimball Diary, South Caroliniana Library, University of South Carolina.

2. Mary Elizabeth Anderson to John Crawford Anderson, 11 June 1862, Moore, *Upcountry South Carolina,* 90.

3. The following is from Blake's "Recollections."

4. Ann[a] [Donaldson] to Parents, 10 October 1863, Anna Donaldson Papers, South Caroliniana Library, University of South Carolina.

5. Williamson, "Seven Ways."

6. Margaret Ann Morris Grimball Diary, 12 May 1862.

7. John Berkly Grimball, "Diary of John Berkly Grimball 1858–1865," *South Carolina Historical Magazine,* 56 (1955): 92–114. For a general study of the subject see Mary Elizabeth Massey, *Refugee Life in the Confederacy* (Baton Rouge: Louisiana State University Press, 1964).

8. The following quotations are taken from the Margaret Ann Morris Grimball Diary.

9. John Berkly Grimball, "Diary of John Berkly Grimball 1858–1865," *South Carolina Historical Magazine,* 57 (1956): 101.

Conclusion

1. For recent accounts of Reconstruction, see Julie Saville, *The Work of Reconstruction: From Slave to Wage Laborer in South Carolina, 1860–1870* (Cambridge, England: Cambridge University Press, 1996), and Richard Zuczek, *State of Rebellion: Reconstruction in South Carolina* (Columbia: University of South Carolina Press, 1996).

2. Ulysses S. Grant, *Memoirs and Selected Letters* (New York: Library of America, 1990), 735.

3. William Tecumseh Sherman, *Memoirs of General W. T. Sherman* (New York: Library of America, 1990), 705.

WORKS CITED

Government Documents

Court of General Sessions. Spartanburg, South Carolina. Columbia, South Carolina Department of Archives and History.

Pickens, Andrew. Official Correspondence, 1860–62. Columbia, South Carolina Department of Archives and History.

Spartanburg District Magistrates and Freeholders Court, 1824–1865. South Carolina Department of Archives and History.

Toland, Elihu. Partisan Rangers. Service Records. Columbia, South Carolina Department of Archives and History.

United States, South Carolina, Spartanburg Population Census for 1850 and 1860.

United States, South Carolina, Spartanburg Slave Census for 1850 and 1860.

Archival Sources

"12 We Wonders." Spartanburg Court of General Sessions. Benjamin Finch 1866 #6. South Carolina Department of Archives and History. Columbia, South Carolina.

Ashmore, John Durant. Papers. Caroliniana Library, University of South Carolina. Columbia, South Carolina.

Blake, William Kennedy. "Recollections." Southern Historical Collection, Special Collections, Wilson Library, University of North Carolina.

"Broadside." Amateur Concert, 23 September 1861, Ladies Relief Association Spartanburg. Caroliniana Library, University of South Carolina. Columbia, South Carolina.

Chesnut-Miller-Manning Papers. South Carolina Historical Society. Charleston, South Carolina.

Donaldson, Anna. Papers. The Caroliniana Library, University of South Carolina. Columbia, South Carolina.

Farrow, T. Stobo. Papers. The Caroliniana Library, University of South Carolina. Columbia, S.C.

Grimball, Margaret Ann Morris. Diary, 1860–66. Southern Historical Collection, Special Collections, Wilson Library, University of North Carolina.

Harris, Emily Lyles. Journals. Special Collections, Dacus Library, Winthrop University.

Keller, J. A. Papers. Caroliniana Library, University of South Carolina. Columbia, South Carolina.

Magrath, Andrew C. Papers. Letters Received and Sent, 1865. Columbia, South Carolina Department of Archives and History.

Minutes. Spartanburg Methodist Sunday School Relief Society, 1861–63, Thomas D. Johnson Papers. Southern Historical Collection, Special Collections, Wilson Library, University of North Carolina.

Moore, Thomas John. Papers. Caroliniana Library, University of South Carolina. Columbia, South Carolina.

Patterson, Samuel Finley. Papers. Duke University Library.

Simpson, Young, Dean and Coleman Families Papers, 1822–90, 1934. Caroliniana Library, University of South Carolina. Columbia, South Carolina.

Smith, Elihu Penquite. Papers. Caroliniana Library, University of South Carolina. Columbia, South Carolina

Smith, Whiteford. Papers. Special Collections, Duke University Library. Durham, North Carolina.

Toland, Elisha. "To the Public." October 20, 1861. Spartanburg Court of General Sessions. Benjamin Finch 1866 #6.

Theses

Gaskins, Sarah Cudd. "The Pioneer Church as an Agency of Social Control: An Analysis of the Record of Two Baptist Churches in South Carolina from 1803–1865 Inclusive." Master's thesis, University of Pittsburg, 1936.

MacArthur, William Joseph. "Antebellum Politics in an Upcountry County: National, State, and Local Issues in Spartanburg County, South Carolina, 1850–1860." Master's thesis, University of South Carolina, 1966.

Articles

Forret, Jeff. "Conflict and the 'Slave Community': Violence among Slaves in Upcountry South Carolina." *Journal of Southern History* 74 (August 2008): 551–88.

Grimball, John Berkly. "Diary of John Berkly Grimball 1858–1865." *South Carolina Historical Magazine,* 56 (1955): 92–114 and 57 (1956): 101.

Otten, James T. "Disloyalty in the Upper Districts of South Carolina during the Civil War." *South Carolina Historical Magazine* 75 (April, 1974): 95–110.

Racine, Philip N. "Emily Lyles Harris: A Piedmont Farmer During the Civil War." *South Atlantic Quarterly* 79 (Autumn 1980): 386–97.

———. "The Slave Catherine and the Kindness of Strangers," *South Carolina Historical Magazine* 113 (April 2012): 146–56.

———. "The Spartanburg District Magistrates and Freeholders Court, 1824–1865." *South Carolina Historical Magazine* 87, (October 1986): 197–212.

———. "The Trials and Tribulations of Jesse Hughey, Free Negro." *The Proceedings of the South Carolina Historical Association,* 1985: 29–39.

Books

Boggs, Doyle. *Historic Spartanburg County: 225 Years of History.* Spartanburg, S.C.: Spartanburg County Historical Association, 2012.

Carlton, David L. *Mill and Town in South Carolina 1880–1920.* Baton Rouge: Louisiana University Press, 1982.

Cauthen, Charles E., ed. *Journals of the South Carolina Executive Councils of 1861 and 1862.* Columbia: University of South Carolina Press, 1956.

———. *South Carolina Goes to War.* Chapel Hill: University of North Carolina Press, 1950.

Craig, Thomas Moore, ed. *Upcountry South Carolina Goes to War: Letters of the Anderson, Brockman, and Moore Families 1853–1865.* Columbia: University of South Carolina Press, 2010.

Dickson, Frank A. *Journeys into the Past: The Anderson Region's Heritage.* N.p., 1975.

Eelman, Bruce W. *Entrepreneurs in the Southern Upcountry: Commercial Culture in Spartanburg, South Carolina, 1845–1880.* Athens: University of Georgia Press, 2008.

Huff, Archie Vernon, Jr. *Greenville: The History of the City and County in the South Carolina Piedmont.* Columbia: University of South Carolina Press, 1995.

Johnson, Michael, and James L. Roark. *Black Masters: A Free Family of Color in the Old South.* Boston: W. W. Norton, 1986.

Landrum, J. B. O. *History of Spartanburg County* (1900). Spartanburg, S.C.: The Reprint Company, 1985.

Massey, Mary Elizabeth. *Refugee Life in the Confederacy.* Baton Rouge: Louisiana State University Press, 1964.

O'Neall, John Belton. *The Negro Law of South Carolina, Collected and Digested by John Belton O'Neall, One of the Judges of the Courts of Law and Errors of the Said State. . . .* Columbia: State Agricultural Society of South Carolina, 1848.

Raboteau, Albert J. *Slave Religion: The "Invisible Institution" in the Antebellum South.* Updated edition. New York: Oxford University Press, 2004.

Racine, Philip N. ed. *Gentlemen Merchants: A Charleston Family's Odyssey, 1828–1870.* Knoxville: University of Tennessee Press, 2008.

———. ed. *Piedmont Farmer: The Journals of David Golightly Harris, 1855–70.* Knoxville: University of Tennessee Press, 1986.

Saville, Julie. *The Work of Reconstruction: From Slave to Wage Laborer in South Carolina, 1860–1870.* Cambridge, U.K.: Cambridge University Press, 1996.

Simpson, R. W. *History of Pendleton District. . . .* (1913). Easley, S.C.: Southern Historical Press, 1978.

Vandiver, Frank E. *Their Tattered Flags.* New York: Harper & Row, 1970.

Wade, Richard. *Slavery in the Cities: The South 1820–1860.* New York: Oxford University Press, 1967.

Wall, Marcus H., Jr. *Spartanburg District Confederate Troops 1861–1865 According to Dr. J. B. O. Landrum.* N.p., 1997.

Wallace, David Duncan. *History of Wofford College, 1854–1949.* Nashville: Vanderbilt University Press, 1951.

Works Progress Administration, *A History of Spartanburg County,* American Guide Series, 1940: Spartanburg, S.C.: The Reprint Company, 1976.

Zuczek, Richard. *State of Rebellion: Reconstruction in South Carolina.* Columbia: University of South Carolina Press, 1996.

INDEX

ABOUT THE AUTHOR

PHILIP N. RACINE is the William R. Kenan, Jr., Professor of History Emeritus at Wofford College in Spartanburg, South Carolina. He is the editor of *The Fiery Trail: A Union Officer's Account of Sherman's Last Campaign, Piedmont Farmer: The Journals of David Golightly Harris, 1855–1870,* and *Gentlemen Merchants: A Charleston Family's Odyssey, 1828–1870,* and author of *Seeing Spartanburg: A History in Images.*